1, 00 - B

S0-ACA-490

J. Robert Oppenheimer

and the Atomic Story

J. Robert Oppenheimer and the Atomic Story

by J. Alvin Kugelmass

decorations by William Metzig

JULIAN MESSNER, INC.　　NEW YORK

Published by Julian Messner, Inc.
8 West 40th Street, New York 18

*Published Simultaneously in Canada
by The Copp Clark Company, Ltd.*

Copyright 1953 by J. Alvin Kugelmass

PRINTED IN THE UNITED STATES OF AMERICA

Library of Congress Catalog Card No. 53-10508

For Elizabeth, Joel and Elise

Contents

1

The Pencil and the Blackboard

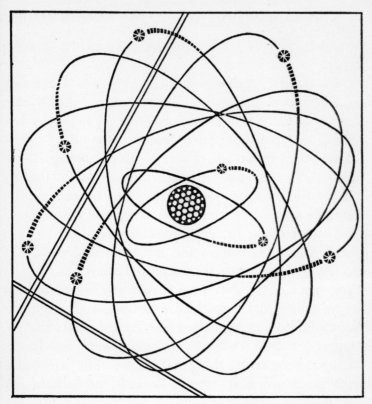

Uranium

A patient-faced man sits just outside the office of the
director of the Institute for Advanced Study at
Princeton, New Jersey. He is no receptionist and
his desk is bare of work. Beneath his jacket—and this is
almost ludicrous considering the scholarly atmosphere of

the Institute—there is the bulge of a gun in the shoulder holster.

On a near-by clothes rack is a brown, flat, chewed-up hat, so famous that it has become a trade-mark of its owner. Newspaper cartoonists need only draw the hat and a few swirling lines to denote whom they have in mind.

The patient man is one of several Atomic Energy Commission detectives assigned to guard the owner of the hat.

If the hat stays late on the rack, then another patient man takes over at the bare desk and sits and waits. Never is the owner of the hat unguarded; he is one of the most valued men of the nation and the Western World—the director of the Institute for Advanced Study.

The office of the director is a spacious affair dominated by a formidable desk piled high with books and pamphlets, a large conference table ringed by taffy-colored chairs and a bank of generous windows overlooking thick woodlands.

The most impressive thing in the office is the blackboard which frequently bears strange symbols and formulas. A little stern sign tells the porter, depending upon the way it is pointing, whether or not the cabalistic-looking signs or equations are to be erased. Once an equation was accidentally rubbed into chalk dust and there was such an outcry that a similar mistake has never again been made.

The director prefers to perch on his desk rather than to sit on his chair. He is very tall—over six feet—and so lean that he has been referred to by geometricians as a refugee from a plane geometry textbook. His eyes are blue, his hair closely cropped in crew-cut fashion, his clothes tweedy and baggy and he looks more like the college senior than the world-famous scientist of forty-nine.

Sitting in an adjacent chair may be Albert Einstein, the great physicist, chatting with the director about his work. Though Einstein is officially retired he still continues to probe the mysteries of the universe with his pencil and his blackboard—even as do many scientists at the unique Institute.

At another time, Edward Mead Earle may be in the director's office. Earle is the famed organizer of the United States Air Force and America's greatest expert on the bombardment of cities. He may go to the blackboard and illustrate a point in his work and the director may make pertinent comments.

Or his visitor may be John van Neumann, builder of the world's fastest electronic "brain," the so-called thinking machine. He and the director are probably discussing knotty electronic problems. The tall, thin man may smile, shrug and say: "John, you know what is best. You just go ahead."

Or there may be George F. Kennan, the former ambassador to the Soviet Union and author of the United States containment policy on Russia. There may be excited talk ranging far back into the history of diplomacy or perhaps no further back than a phase of World War II. Both men fling their arms about as they speak with a high, mutual regard.

There may be Arnold Toynbee, frequently called the "historian's historian." With him, as well, the tall, lean man may converse about the architecture of the Middle Ages or perhaps about some ancient dead religion.

Or there may be T. S. Eliot, the poet, who is discoursing with the director on modern rhymes and sounds which please the ear.

Or there may be anyone of some two hundred learned and famous men in the arts, the sciences and the professions who are under contract at the Institute to do nothing but sit and think about their work. These men, no matter what field they specialize in, look to the director as a colleague, an adviser, a guiding principle and a stimulator—or just as an intelligent listening post.

Into the office there may come a botanist, a social scientist devoted to slum clearance, an architect of international renown, an artist, an expert in the derivation of languages, an economist or a specialist in public health formerly with the United Nations.

With each of these, the unassuming but engaging director will talk, ponder, agree or disagree—and encourage. With each of these, because of his incredible background and grasp, he will speak in the highly specialized language of his visitor.

Who is this very special man who can talk to these very special men and enjoy their high regard and esteem? And what kind of place is this Institute where there are gathered so many men of brilliance in so many fields who are not required to teach or to do anything but pursue their work?

J. Robert Oppenheimer, the owner of the pork-pie hat, is known as "the man who built the atomic bomb," a catch phrase he himself would be the first to deride. To scientists and men of arts the world over, he is not only the "builder" of the bomb and a pioneer in atomic energy, but a master of many languages, a profound student of Oriental philosophies and a seasoned traveler. Too, he is a witty conversationalist, an art collector, a scholar of the drama, a critic of poetry, a colorful writer, a logician, a superb mathematician and an expert in the history of architecture and in the religions of the world.

It is difficult to think of a historical counterpart about whom so many superlatives about so many areas of human learning may be used. Benjamin Franklin comes to mind for he, too, was highly versed in the sciences and the arts. Benvenuto Cellini, the Italian goldsmith, sculptor and scientist comes to mind. Then there was Pliny the Elder, the Roman scholar who lived just after the turn of time from B.C. to A.D. He, as well, was a man well rounded in both science and the arts.

While it is always risky to rank a living man with the dead immortals, yet what Oppenheimer has done will live on forever and will forever profoundly affect the future of all people.

The Institute, which has no official connection with Princeton University, though it is near by, was founded in 1930 by Louis Bamberger, a New Jersey department store magnate, and Mrs. Felix Fuld who set up a fund of some twenty-one million dollars.

Simply stated, the Institute was established as a place where men of vision could work out their ideas without having to expend their energies and time at teaching.

The Institute was thus designed as a kind of retreat, an intellectual monastery to which men of stature from all over the world, regardless of race, nationality or creed, could come to think their fondest dreams through to a conclusion—without the need to worry about money or to do other work of any kind.

Some of the members of the Institute are life members. Of late, though, the trend has been, as Oppenheimer puts it, to invite people "who have something to communicate" to come for a year. During this period they can gather their wits together and work out conclusions they had always hoped to have time to reach.

Oppenheimer, or Oppy, as he is known to his friends and colleagues, came to the Institute as director late in 1947. His most important role as director is that he can at times suggest to one thinker in one branch of thought a line of research going on in still another branch.

He is thus a kind of one-man clearing house of the vast fund of the known, a kind of amalgam for many areas of science and research. He has of course subsidiary roles as director, but being the cultural touchstone for his colleagues is his favorite and most important task.

As is true of all science and the arts, the Institute knows

no national frontiers. On the staff are people from the Netherlands, Belgium, Germany, Japan, Poland, Czecho-slovakia, Denmark, Norway, India, Palestine, China, New Zealand, Australia—a veritable United Nations of culture and research.

The men of stature from all over the world who come to the Institute as members embrace almost every area of learning, though preponderately they are men of science.

Formally, the Institute is divided into three schools: the school of humanistic studies, the school of economics and politics and the school of mathematics. Oppenheimer, primarily a physicist, tries to devote most of his free after-noons to the school of mathematics, for mathematics is the fulcrum of physics. Theoretical physics is Oppy's first love, though he is accomplished in many fields.

When Oppy is home, which is only about half the time, he and his wife Kitty, an expert in plant life and a former student of his, live at an exquisite, two-hundred-year-old farmhouse called Olden Manor. The house, a spacious affair with huge, lofty rooms and numerous fireplaces, goes with his job as director and is set in the lovely and historic New Jersey countryside.

The Oppenheimers have two children—Peter, born in 1941, and Toni, a girl, born in 1945. Peter is showing a bent for science and mathematics, which is not surprising considering his home environment.

Mrs. Oppenheimer maintains a beautiful greenhouse where she experiments in her branch of science, the physiology of plants. She also holds a degree in mycology, the branch of botany dealing with fungi. Mrs. Oppenheimer entertains with a minimum of formality. The Oppenheimers are among the most gregarious people in the Princeton environs and rarely an evening goes by, when he is at home, that a dozen or more distinguished people are not chattering away in the vast living room.

The Oppenheimers live simply. They like good music, go shopping together for groceries in near-by Princeton, worry about the cuts, aches, sprains and illnesses of their children and are as down to earth in their attitudes about weather and neighbors as any average family. Oppy has given his babies bottles in the small hours of the night and he plays with them at their games. He frets about their rashes and colds and keeps after them to brush their teeth and mind their manners. For a man who is called a genius, he certainly displays all the attitudes and tendencies of a typical parent. In addition to his job at the Institute, Oppenheimer, until recently, was also chairman of the Atomic Energy Commission's General Advisory Committee, the highest scientific group within the A.E.C., and is adviser to the United States atomic delegation to the United Nations. He also takes time out to fly to England to lecture at Cambridge University or to confer in Chicago with a conclave of atomic physicists.

There are times when he makes plane reservations for the East, West, North and South so that he can leave from one place for the next at a moment's notice. His switchoard exchange at the Institute, Princeton 2580, may eceive in a single day calls from the North Atlantic Treaty Organization in France, the Atomic Energy Commission n Washington, a Japanese scholar in Tokyo who is con-ronted with a knotty problem in physics and wishes to sk his friend Oppy's advice.

He may shuttle back and forth by plane to NATO wice in two weeks to confer with generals of the Allied lefense and in between may sandwich a hurried flight o a California university to inspect a new cyclotron and o suggest improvements.

The busy life and the high posts did not come about .ccidentally. Oppy—and he cringes when this is men-ioned—was a boy genius and from then on developed into a man genius. He did this through fierce and unremitting tudy and a gigantic curiosity about the world.

He is linguist, poet, scientist, traveler, connoisseur of rt and architecture, physicist, mineralogist and botanist. He is also sportsman of no mean quality. Well known as a ecturer and teacher, he is considered a philosopher of the atomic era as well as the "man who built the atomic bomb."

When Oppenheimer speaks, the press listens and reports on page one. His influence is felt in Congress, in Parliament, the French Chamber of Deputies and in the Kremlin. When he makes a statement about the use of atomic energy or about what he considers unnecessary secrecy, the world reacts rapidly in its press, its magazines and its books.

He did not acquire this authority lightly. For his background, his devotion to his work and the colossal task he undertook during war pressures to beat the enemy to the atomic bomb is an epic in concentrated scholarship and drive and intellect.

The story of his youth is an incredible one and full of high adventure—in books. His later years as a student and teacher and rapidly developing genius is even more stimulating. And his fulfillment as the architect of the atomic age—the man who pulled the switch to split the atom—is perhaps the most exciting thing that can befall any man.

When the legendary Prometheus brought the fire from the heavens to give it to man on earth, it was not nearly as staggering an accomplishment as when J. Robert Oppenheimer in 1942, at the age of thirty-eight, took over the formidable dream of making the split atom come to pass.

What manner of boy was this, what manner of man was this, that he was selected to head up the vast conglomeration of genius which made possible the dawning of the new era—the atomic era?

2

The Crucible

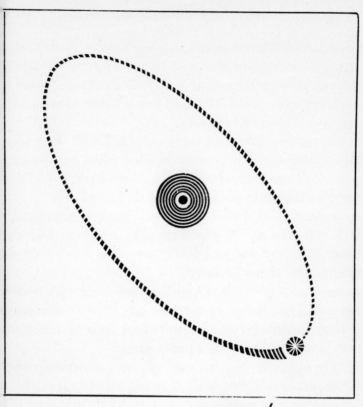

Hydrogen

When Oppenheimer speaks of his childhood he
winces. He is not at all fond of his recollections.
"I was," he says, "an unctuous, repulsively good
little boy." Then he shudders.

Apparently he was. When he was five his grandfather

gave him a gift of a small collection of rocks. With a fervo
unusual for boys of that age, he soon learned to lisp th
difficult geological names of each rock specimen. "I remem
ber being quite proud, though I'm not today, of such unac
customed behavior for a boy."

His parents, however, were delighted with their scho.
arly young son. They never minded when he refused t
play with other children in Riverside Park, New Yor
City, on the banks of the beautiful Hudson River.

"I don't think I ever got dirty," he says reminiscentl
and with distaste. "Nor do I recall ever playing with chi
dren. Why this was so I don't know, but it certainly wa
neither normal nor civilized."

As wealth goes, the Oppenheimers were very well t
do. Julius, the father, of German extraction, was a gentle
scholarly man who soon began to look upon his precociou
son, as Oppy puts it, "as a public trust."

"He began to plan to turn me into something wort
while, preferably in science. I repaid his confidence in m
by developing an unpleasing ego which I am sure must hav
affronted both children and adults who were unfortunat
enough to come into contact with me," he recalls wit
horror.

The family appeared to have everything it wanted. Th
—coupled with a doting father and a gentle, loving mothe
who demanded only good decorum and manners from he
son—did not prepare him, Oppy says, for the grim realitie
of life.

"My life as a child never fitted me for the fact that the
world is full of cruel and bitter things."

Oppy's mother, Ella, nee Freedman, gave birth to her
firstborn on April 22, 1904. Filled with joy and pride,
his parents never dreamed that their son was to make come
true a dream of the twentieth century which scientists at
the time of his birth were sure was either impossible or
would not occur for several hundreds of years: the splitting
of the atom and the release of atomic energy to the world.
Mrs. Oppenheimer was a skilled and passionate painter
who shared with her husband a deep love of music. The
boy was thus brought up in a household which knew no
poverty and was filled with all the cultural delights the
fond parents could visit upon him. At an early age he knew
enough about the great classical composers to recognize
even obscure selections from the great symphonies. Too,
he shared in the painting lessons his mother gave neighborhood children as a hobby.

The boy was always impeccably dressed in the best
fashion of the period. Since the district was a rich and
fashionable one, the elementary school which he attended
was one of the best in the city. Riverside Drive, at that
time, was considered the smartest street not only in New
York City but across the nation.

The year in which Oppenheimer was born was a time
of optimism concerning prosperity and peace. There had
not been a major war since 1870, the Franco-Prussian War,
and except for the mild and short Spanish-American War

and the Boer War in South Africa, most of the civilize
world believed that nations were too well established an
civilized ever again to resort to armed conflict.

England was content with its mighty empire and indee
was at its zenith. France had recovered from the turmo
following 1870 and was deeply involved in culture. Ger
many was pushing forward its scientific adventures an
its trade. Japan was emerging from its feudalism. Italy
following the withdrawal in 1870 of French troops fror
Rome, also was a nation with dreams of reviving its ancien
classical culture.

In 1904, following the great industrial revolution an
the use of machines in factories, the United States Paten
Office was deluged with new inventions. Stories in th
more lurid press told about experiments with a heavier
than-air flying machine. A Frenchman, Louis Blériot, jus
a few years previously had crossed the English Channe
in a flying boat, but few paid much attention to it. In th
living rooms of the civilized world men said to each othe
"Sure, flying will come, but not in my time or yours."

It seems long ago, but it was not. Women wore big ha
and hobble skirts. They did not smoke either in public c
in private. Men wore whiskers or great mustaches. Th
streets were cobblestoned and horse trolleys began to mak
the day hideous with their din. It was a good time for th
Western World, however, for with peace and the suret
of peace men began to turn more and more to cultur
and to seek a better understanding of the life about then

The Oppenheimer family was no exception. The parents ied to see to it that the home was a place of beauty and in. There were flowers in the house, good music and n hour or two spent with the boy. Life then was unhurried nd there were far fewer outside attractions. This made or more of a home upbringing. Julius Oppenheimer was ngrossed with history and spent much time telling his son bout Europe.

Soon the boy became obsessed with the architecture f European homes and churches and great monuments. .t an early age he announced to his parents that he was oing to be an architect. His parents told him that they ad no objection and liked the idea. Soon the home began o be flooded with books on architecture, which the boy ould barely read, and with prints and photographs of great rchitectural masterpieces.

But before he was seven he changed his mind. Now he /as going to be a poet. Then the home was flooded with olumes of the great classical poets and Oppy was scrib-ling his childish verses on unlimited pads of paper supplied im by his mother.

His toys were unlike the toys of other children. For ne thing, he had an exquisitely fine microscope made 1 Germany that had been especially ordered from abroad. Ie developed a butterfly collection and soon learned the .atin names of his specimens.

His collection of stamps, none very expensive, was, how-ver, extensive. Everytime his father presented him with

a new stamp for his albums he proceeded to tell him th
history of the nation from which the stamp had emanated

He also had a fine collection of dried flowers and leave
and these, too, he developed into an avenue of knowledg
by learning the names, the species and the countries c
climates to which they were native.

He paid scant attention to ordinary toys such as skates. '
just never knew the pleasure of roller skating," he say
"Nor did I even know how to ride a bike until a few yea
ago. Apparently, such joys had no attraction for me simpl
because it was the routine for other children."

His greatest pleasure was to fish a drop out of a cup c
soup, place it on his microscope and watch the strange bug
appear in the bathed, bright light. He would then run t
his books and try to determine the classifications of th
bugs.

Then painting caught his fancy as he watched his mothe
at her canvas. Nothing would do now but that he woul
be a great painter. "Somehow, I never longed to be a fire
man or a policeman," he says, with his wry humor. "Yes,
was one of those nasty little children who enjoyed, c
professed to enjoy, an art exhibit to which my mother, i
her earnestness to help me, took me."

Soon he was working away at his own little easel an
had his own little box of oils and brushes. Soon, too, h
was discussing art theories with his parents and indulgin
in free expression with them. They rarely talked to hir
as a child but more as an equal, as an adult. His father se

om talked about his business affairs but preferred to dis-
uss art, history, culture of any kind. The friends who
ropped in for dinner and an evening of talk were also
om the arts or the sciences.

The father became more and more obsessed as he
atched the boy take to the arts and sciences with an
se and maturity which was astonishing to friends and
eighbors. What had been a traditional fond hope now
ecame a passion. He was sure the boy had something
nusual and he was resolved that Oppy would have nothing
ut the best so that his potentials could be developed. He
esolved to enter the boy in the Ethical Culture School, an
istitution operated by the Ethical Culture Society.

The school was a unique place for unique children. It
ppears that all through his life Oppy was to have associa-
ons with unique institutions.

The Ethical Culture School was founded in 1878 by
Dr. Felix Adler for the six boys and two girls who were
t the top of their classes in the Midtown Elementary
chool on Central Park West, New York City, a very
xpensive thoroughfare and a favorite street for the pro-
essional, well-to-do classes. Dr. Adler also recruited chil-
ren from the Fieldston School in Riverdale, Westchester
County, another expensive area favored by wealthy intel-
ectuals.

It was merely an experiment. It was Dr. Adler's thought,
ne shared by many educators of the period and still held
y many of them, that exceptionally bright children should

not be held back by the slower ones. It was believed tha the child who could absorb more in less time should ne have to wait for those who were slower.

This unusual school had a second characteristic. Accord ing to the brochure of the time, "it is to help children di cover and develop their unique possibilities of mind an character and to promote their growth through sensitiv response to fundamental aspects of society and the cultur in which they live."

A prime and basic reason for the formation of the schoo was the fact that many parents of many faiths in New Yor City and elsewhere were determined that all the faiths ha good to offer. And they felt that "being able to live to gether, regardless of race, color or creed," was the mos beautiful thing in life. They resolved therefore to foun a school where this "teaching of living together" could b made part of every course. It was a noble aspiration and i many respects it has been realized.

The school was also a very hardheaded place in the sens that such courses as weaving, sewing, cooking and arts an crafts were important parts of the curriculum. The school administrator felt that these were some of the rudimen of everyday life.

The Ethical Culture School was to have a profoun effect on Oppy's life, his way of thinking, his approac to people and problems and his revulsion against discrim ination of any kind. It is thus important to dwell somewha

n the scope and the intention of the school, for it was—
nd still is—unique in the educational system.

The school taught the dignity and the worth of manual
bor. Dr. Adler knew that very little is done automatically,
ough much of the world's work is done by the machine.
machine, for example, he pointed out, cannot fix a door-
ell. A machine cannot cook in the sense that it can prepare
e ingredients of a savory meal and put in just so much
lt.

One of the great difficulties in getting the school started
as finding teachers who understood the experimental
oncepts of education. Finally Henry A. Kelly, a curator
the Museum of Natural History in Worcester, Massa-
usetts, was selected to head the new school. Kelly was
valuable and got the school off to a good start simply
cause he had been working with children in just the
nd of work envisioned by Dr. Adler. He had been using
e children of a near-by school to help him classify and
entify museum specimens. He had taught these children
at working with stones, bugs and leaves was not only
lucational but fun.

Ethical culture schools have expanded across the more
opulated sections of the nation and the enrollment is in
e thousands. Many hundreds of distinguished citizens
ve been graduated by Ethical culture schools and look
ck with a conscious awareness to the courses of training
hich helped them to help themselves think.

Not long after Oppy was enrolled at Ethical Culture, h
began to learn languages with an amazing facility. Wit
the aid of his teachers and by himself at home, he concen
trated on Greek and the Romance languages—Frencl
Spanish and Italian. At this point, he said, he was goir
to be a classicist who would spend the rest of his life study
ing and teaching languages and the history of language

Most especially, he became enchanted with Gree
mythology, and its stories about the war between Ather
and Sparta, the taking of the Golden Fleece and the fir
Olympic games which were designed to try and mal
peace between and among the warring Greek city-state

He also studied the great Greek poets, philosopher
dramatists and playwrights. He was then only seven. Pla
outdoors still did not interest him and he became mo
excited about the rhyme forms used by the ancient Greci
poet-balladeers than about any kind of ball game. H
learned to chant ancient Greek songs of victory or defe
and his mother would pick the notes out on the piano an
write them down for him. The neighboring children mu
have considered him the counterpart of today's "worm"
"grind."

Then, for some reason he cannot recall, he turned ba
to his interest in rocks. He studied the deep scratches an
formations in the rocks in Central Park and this, at lea
got him outdoors quite a lot.

He enjoyed his classes at Ethical Culture where l
continued to write poetry, to paint landscapes, and to dra

beautiful buildings and universities such as he would build when he was playing at being an architect.

Meantime his parents became excited over their latest offspring, born on August 14, 1912, a baby brother, Frank Freedman Oppenheimer.

The newcomer naturally created a great deal of attention. Oppy, who was almost nine years old, shared with his parents the complex business of caring for and playing with the baby. Soon the baby became a commonplace as he crawled and toddled about, and Oppy turned his attention back to his first love, rocks, a curiosity in which his brother as yet did not appear to participate.

Oppy embarked on a correspondence with professors of geology throughout the country and built up a fine library devoted to rocks. He soon learned to use a typewriter and this, together with an amazing command of language, deceived many of the experts with whom he communicated. Had they seen his youthful scrawl, perhaps they would have been more amazed, so lucid and knowledgeable were his letters.

Not long afterward a professor with whom Oppy corresponded put his name up for membership in the New York Mineralogical Club, a group composed of both laymen and experts, adults all, who made rocks their passionate study.

At the age of eleven, because of his superb grasp of mineralogy, J. Robert Oppenheimer was duly informed by mail that he had been elected a member of the club.

During summer vacations at the family's lovely summer home at Islip, New York, he roamed far and wide collecting mineral specimens which he charted, catalogued and labeled. His room soon resembled a laboratory rather than a typical boy's room.

He maintained a steady correspondence with club officials and members, and to his own amazement and his father's delight, at the age of twelve he was invited to deliver a lecture at the next meeting of the Mineralogical Club.

Family friends could not express their astonishment and Oppy himself lost some of his bravado and felt queasy. He asked his father to notify the club that he was ill or to tell them the truth about his age. But his father would have none of it. Julius Oppenheimer was a proud man.

The night of the date set for the lecture arrived. Accompanied by his mother and his father, Oppy went to the club's quarters which were then situated in a West Side New York hotel.

They were greeted by an usher. He couldn't seem to understand that the boy of twelve was to be the principal speaker and that he was J. Robert Oppenheimer. Mrs Oppenheimer laughed with pleasure while the father beamed and finally convinced the usher who led the trio to the chairman for the evening's meeting.

There was some consternation when Oppy, prepared with an address, went behind the little rostrum. When he began to speak there was a flurry of talk in the audience

Then there was a burst of applause. Oppy almost lost his aplomb but went bravely on, while both parents beamed with pleasure.

He says it is doubtful, such was the amazement and amusement, whether anyone paid much attention to his talk which was based on the rich minerals which form the bedrock of Manhattan Island but which are not valuable enough to disturb the expensive real estate built on top of them.

However, his paper was reprinted in the infrequent publications of the club. It was the first time anything he said or wrote had actually appeared in print. He mourns the loss of the only copy he had.

Not long after Oppy delivered his first lecture, his interest sharply turned to chemistry. His parents gave him his head and let him roam intellectually wherever he wished.

Chemistry opened up new worlds to him. He saw a kind of orderliness in nature all about him as revealed by chemistry. As he puts it today: "It was very exciting when I first learned of the atomic theory, of valence and the periodic system—those wonderful regularities which reveal the deep order and the rationality of nature." What he means, in effect, is that he was terribly excited to discover the integrity that exists in natural laws and how full of common sense natural laws are.

By the time he reached his senior year at Ethical Culture, he had become conversationally eloquent in Latin. He composed actual sonnets in the old, lovely dead language and confounded his teachers who by then constituted a brilliant faculty.

In his senior year he also mastered Greek for which he had formed an early love. He spoke a fluent Greek that was astonishing to hear from a small boy and he read Plato, Homer and Sophocles without benefit of a dictionary.

He also mastered French by the time he was a senior and his Spanish and Italian were as native to him as English. All of this proficiency sounds well-nigh miraculous. Yet Thomas Babington Macaulay, the great British essayist, wrote a history of the world in Greek when he was seven. Oppy likes to point this out so that he might take the curse off his own youthful erudition which somehow to many persons sounds like bad taste.

So facile was he with languages that he would write poetry in French, translate it into Greek and then from the Greek render it into Italian to see whether he still could retain the same iambic pentameters. He is not sure today, but he thinks some of his teachers were not only fascinated by his ease at studies but also revolted. "No one likes a cocky little boy even if he's not really cocky," he says. "Just knowing so much sounds cocky at that age."

He was a lonely boy during those years at Ethical Culture. While it was the kind of school which had no extracurricular sports and encouraged the precocious so that he was among his own kind, yet he found himself far too busy to make friends and lead the normal social life of a boy. Sometimes he was terribly lonely but he didn't know it until he was much older and began to mellow.

Too, he was shy. This may have stemmed from the world of books in which he lived and also from the fact that his mother had stressed so greatly the importance of good manners. He always wanted to be sure of his manners. Though he spoke up readily enough when classwork was in question, it was not cocksureness, as many thought, but certainty of his subject that made him express himself freely. He would have been horrified to know at that age that he was considered brazen for he felt anything but that.

Nor did the fact that he was not athletic help him make friends. All his contemporaries, no matter how badly they did at sports, played baseball, tennis or soccer. He had no inclination toward sports and even when he did try them he found he did them badly and didn't enjoy them.

His parents, scholarly and bookish, did not trouble themselves about his lack of play. They much preferred to have him associate with a classmate who had the same interests he had: rocks, languages, chemistry and music.

His father felt so keenly about his progress that he resolved that Oppy would not waste a summer vacation in undisciplined study. He retained Augustus Klock, a science teacher at Ethical Culture, to be the boy's tutor at their summer home at Islip.

Under Klock's direction Mr. Oppenheimer set up a complete chemical laboratory and thousands of dollars were spent completing the private summer workshop. When it was finished it was a good facsimile of some of the better college laboratories.

Klock and Oppy went to work and kept regular school hours. After classes they would walk and discuss the stirring events of the day. World War I was on and it appeared that the United States would soon be involved, in order to repel the aggression of the Kaiser. Frank, of course, attended all the courses as an interested bystander and was frequently filled in on what he could not readily grasp. He, too, was able to pick up the rudiments of what Klock taught and, like many another younger brother, watched and listened with admiration while Klock and Oppy held forth on chemistry, history and current events.

Within six weeks Oppy completed a full year's work in chemistry. Klock, using the ethical culture method of concentrating on laboratory work rather than on textbooks, was amazed. Mr. Oppenheimer was pleased at Oppy's remarkable progress and stirred with pride when Klock, a man not given to extravagant phrases, said: "Your son, I sincerely believe, will be a genius."

His father was so elated that he purchased as a gift for Oppy, a boy's dream—a twenty-seven-foot sloop. She was to be all his own, his father said, and he could name her what he wished.

Characteristically, Oppy named the boat *Trimethy*, a diminutive for the chemical word trimenhylene chloride. Klock roared when he attended the christening of the sloop and watched Oppy smash a laboratory bottle full of some foul-smelling chemical against the bow.

The boy began to love the boat and it was good for him. For one thing, he grew tanned and began to fill out as his appetite improved. For another, it brought him into contact with a refreshing and wholesome sport and he soon began to enjoy the challenge of his boyish muscles against the ropes during rough weather on Long Island Sound. Frank was his first mate and enjoyed saluting his captain and following his instructions with a naval dash and crispness.

Oppy was graduated from Ethical Culture School at the head of his class. He received *A*'s in every one of his grades and delivered the graduation address. His subject, he recalls, was highly philosophical and very dull. His graduation picture shows that he has not changed very much: there is the lean head of a greyhound or perhaps the profile that may be found on a medieval coin; there is the intense glance which does not lack for humor; there is the gangling frame of the boy who showed promise of becoming the gangling man.

There then arose a vast debate in the home of the Oppenheimers. What to do for the boy now? What courses should he take and, as Oppy puts it, "My parents wondered what school I should honor by my presence."

Klock was consulted. "True," he said. "The boy has a vast capacity for learning. But that does not mean he can produce. He is a magnificent student but that does not mean he will do anything with what he learns. Let's let up on that word 'genius' for a long while."

Mr. Oppenheimer had a solution, albeit a temporary one. "I will take my son to Europe. He deserves it and besides it will give both of us a chance to talk and to think about his future. His future is too important to be decided just like that—on a moment's deliberation. He must be carefully groomed."

Off to Europe went father and son. The boy spent a great deal of his time in the engine room discussing revolutions of motors, tides and the wonderful Gulf Stream.

When Oppy returned to New York he came back with a stack of notes on the baroque architecture he had seen, and with specimens of rocks he had gotten from formations in France. He had also dropped a stone from the top of the leaning Tower of Pisa in Italy and had done mathematical calculations on the angle; he saw the Tower of London where many famous Britons had been hanged, and had copious notes on the ropes that were used in that day; and he saw the spot in Greece where Leonidas had stood off the Persians in the suicidal Battle of Thermopylae and where Lord Byron, his favorite poet, had died.

The boy came home full of memories, notes and wondrous associations with all he had read and studied. History, of a sudden, came alive to him and developed a third dimension, that of reality. He was in Rotterdam and saw where Erasmus had been born and in Frankfort, Germany, where Goethe had lived. People and incidents, which had taken on form only in his books, now became very real things. He was now resolved to be a classicist and said he would like to spend his life teaching the wonders of the civilizations that had once thrived and perished.

But again, though he was a formidable boy with stately ideas, he still remained a boy. The role of the teacher of ancient civilization lost interest for him and one day he said: "I want to go to Harvard."

Klock was called in. He said cautiously: "Harvard is a very good school. Let the boy find his way."

Oppy was enrolled at Harvard in 1923, at the age of nineteen. It was a young age but he had the credentials and successfully passed the entrance examinations.

At Harvard he completed the four-year course in three years. His first year, however, was a lonely one.

Then his wit and humor began to be made manifest. This, coupled with his high intellect and his high grades, soon won for him a host of friends among the faculty and the students.

Beneath the benison of friends who truly liked him and respected him, he warmed—and for the first time in his life he became, as he says, "a social animal." Wherever he went he found kindred interests. He began to talk animatedly about history, about physics, about speed and flight, and he found to his pleasure that there were many other minds at Harvard which dwelled on the same ideas.

Evenings he invited classmates to his handsome rooms where they drank beer, talked politics and culture, discussed girls and professors, told jokes and played pranks. Occasionally he stayed up all night indulging in the immemorial dormitory gab fests about life, love and literature.

He joined no social clubs, no fraternities, no societies and engaged in no extracurricular activities. He received two bids to fraternities because of his outstanding grades but he declined both simply because he was listed as a Jew at both frat houses. He had registered as a member of the Ethical Culture Society but the fraternities refused to recognize this. Oppy says he would not have joined anyhow but he wished to put his declination on the grounds that most fraternities at the more expensive colleges appeared to discriminate against Catholics, Jews and Negroes.

During his second year at Harvard Oppy was given the opportunity to select from a long list of elective courses and was asked to choose his major. He chose chemistry and was sorry later on for he felt that his chief interest lay in physics. At this time he was taking seven courses while most sophomores were taking only four or five.

He still felt that he wasn't going ahead fast enough and went to see Percy Bridgman, professor of physics.

"I'm a soph, sir," he said to the renowned teacher, "and I just don't have enough to do."

"How many courses are you taking?" Bridgman asked. "Besides," he added, "I take on only graduate students if that's why you came to see me."

"Well, sir," and Oppy swallowed, "I'm taking seven

courses and I majored in chemistry which I think was a mistake." Then he added: "But they all seem so elementary, my courses do."

The professor cleared his throat with embarrassment. While Oppy had been honest in saying that he was running far ahead of his schedule, that kind of talk sounded distasteful and bragging.

"That seems very unusual for your age. Most boys would like more free time. Why not sit in at my class and we'll see what happens."

Oppy went to Bridgman's class and to his horror he saw that all the students were much older. All had been graduated from one college or another and were taking postgraduate courses in physics with Bridgman and other noted physics teachers.

At first Bridgman was aghast to discover that his new student was all thumbs in the physics laboratory. Oppy fumbled, broke equipment, could not make experiments come to pass when by all the natural laws they should have.

The great teacher shook his head sadly and wondered at his own kindness. But then he began to be impressed. While Oppy could not perform an experiment properly and with good manual dexterity, he understood far better than most of the other members of the class the theory behind the experiment.

Soon Bridgman became more and more impressed as Oppy began to go beyond the experiment itself and to understand the next steps—just by talking and thinking out loud.

This was a valuable experience for Oppy. He began to understand himself better and to recognize that while he might not be able to repair a car properly because he could not handle tools as he should, he did understand the theory of what should be fixed and how it should be fixed.

It was to be this lack of operative skill with tools and with actual laboratory implements that was to turn Oppy to theoretical physics and to his paper work—and later on, to his administrative and co-ordinating job at building the Big Firecracker.

Oppy looks back at his years at Harvard as among the most exciting of his life, the most stimulating, and the period when he found himself and found what he wanted to do.

He read Dante in his spare time in the original Italian and confounded his teachers. But here he was no longer a boy and his grasp was not distasteful to the giants who were his teachers. He also read many other books which he had always wanted to read but for which he hadn't had time.

He spoke with Chinese students and traded them instruction in French for similar introductions to the mysteries of the Chinese alphabet.

During his third year at Harvard he took a total of ten courses, a phenomenal number. He registered for six, elected to attend four more and took examinations in all.

He loved examinations. To him they were a challenge, a kind of counterpoise, an assault on his intellect which had to be met.

His reputation at Harvard, which is still legendary, has it that he liked nothing better on a hot day than to curl up with Jean's *Dynamical Theory of Gases*.

He became a kind of professors' pet and often visited at the home of Bridgman and the late, great Alfred North Whitehead. There he would argue theoretical physics until his elders told him to go home. But again, by this time he was not the insufferable boy intellect, but the grown student with a good mind.

He was graduated from Harvard University *summa cum laude*. He was the valedictorian of his class and achieved the highest grades yet recorded at the great and ancient college.

Not bad at all for a boy with a good background who had everything he wanted. This somehow destroys the illusion that it is only the earnest boy from the slums who makes good and runs away with his class. It may be a better story when the slum boy does it, but it does not detract from the rich boy when he does it.

3

One Plus One Equals Two

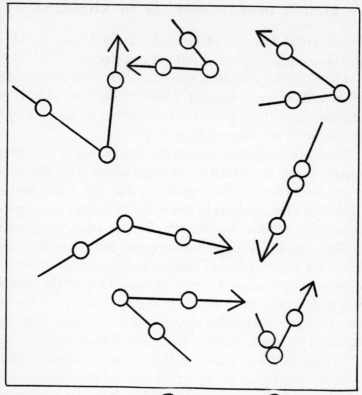

Brownian Motion

I n 1926 Oppy *graduated from Harvard and his parents*
attended the commencement exercises and saw their
son run away with a great many of the scholastic honors. None of the athletic honors came his way. His cap
looked too large for him and his gown dangled all about

him in folds. He says of himself: "I could have gotten a job on a fairly well-sized farm as a scarecrow."

His old tutor, Augustus Klock, attended the commencement exercises and he said with wry humor: "He is so brilliant that I think this is the first exercise he has ever had. It is good to see him outdoors."

Professor Bridgman, before the faculty began its stately march in cap and gown to its assigned place on the platform, leaned forward to a colleague and said: "You know, J. Robert Oppenheimer is due today to deliver the *summa cum laude* address. Let me tell you one story about him.

"He was at my home one evening and I was showing him some photos taken of temples constructed several hundreds of years before Christ was born. One of the photos I showed him was of a temple at Segeste, Sicily, you know, one of those out-of-the-way places which had been influenced by Rome during the Roman Empire.

"Well, that boy leaned forward and said that he was sorry to contradict me about the date of the construction of the temple. He said that he could tell by the number of columns supporting the structure and by the flutings on the columns themselves that the temple had been built at least fifty years before I said it had been."

Both men shook with laughter. Bridgman said that Oppenheimer was destined to go on and tear down preconceived notions. "That boy will either shake up physics or the world," he said. He was correct in both his assumptions for the "boy" was to do both.

ONE PLUS ONE EQUALS TWO

Following his graduation from Harvard, Oppy had a long talk with his father. "I want you to do whatever you want to do," said the proud man. "As a matter of fact, I'll settle some money on you to show my faith in you." It is estimated that Oppy came in for something like fifty thousand dollars to use as he wished.

Armed with his honors from Harvard and incited with a desire to learn more, such was the curiosity that gripped him, he immediately enrolled at Cambridge University in England. He sought out his favorite professors who naturally gave him letters of recommendation. With these—and of course his Harvard degree plus the honors which had been heaped upon him at the commencement exercises—he had no difficulty in obtaining an immediate admission. He selected physics as his course of study.

One of the most characteristic comments of Oppy's life at Harvard was made by himself when he was asked to send along a phrase which would best describe his stay at the university: In the yearbook for 1926 there is this sparse phrase, all he had to say about himself: "In college three years as an undergraduate."

No bleaker, no lonelier, no sadder expression could be coined. Here was a man destined to cause an upheaval in the scientific life of man and perhaps in the history of nations, and yet all he had to say about himself in the yearbook of the university where he obtained his fundamentals was that he had spent some time at that place.

He entered the famous Cavendish Laboratories at Cambridge University as an equal, not an assistant. The deal had been arranged by Professor Bridgman, his sponsor and admirer.

During one eventful year at Cambridge Oppy had dozens of discussions with the late, great Lord Ernest Rutherford, the eminent physicist who did so much work on the components of matter; with Niels Bohr, who was to work with Rutherford on what is known as the Rutherford-Bohr atom; with the famed Max Born, who was greatly taken up with the youthful, intense student-thinker and his theories about the structure of matter; with P. A. M. Dirac, the great physicist, the kindly, gentle expert in the mathematics of space, who later was to join the Institute as a member.

It was a full, crowded year and one that Oppy looks back upon with nostalgia and affection. Somehow, he feels that it was during that year that most of the talk leading up to the splitting of the atom was about as close to the final denouement as it had ever come.

While Oppy was at Cambridge Professor Max Born urged him to continue his studies at the University of Göttingen in Germany. Göttingen was then regarded as the most advanced institution in the world devoted to higher mathematics. Born looked upon Oppenheimer as his protégé and wanted him to come into contact with the men he felt had the most to offer.

"You will find the most advanced thinking in the world in Göttingen. Go there," the kindly man urged. Oppy was grateful and the two soon established a fine rapport—one, the master, the other, the pupil, but on a basis of close friendship.

Born worked along with Oppenheimer at Cambridge, coached him, scolded him, held him in check, quarreled with him, but always treated him as an equal.

It was now 1927; Oppenheimer was only twenty-three years old and he was consorting with the mightiest mathematicians of the time.

At Göttingen, accompanied by Born, Oppenheimer, with his facility for language, soon began to speak German like a native and the night was filled with theory, talk, singing and joy. Oppy soon found an element in his life he had missed at Harvard: he could foregather with his colleagues, could partake of fun and a stein of beer and make merry with them.

His loneliness at Harvard probably stemmed simply from the fact that he was so much further advanced intellectually than his classmates that their serious talk or their sport or their fun left him cold. Here, however, in Göttingen, where all about him there were historical associations, intricate mathematical brains, and a kind of joyousness in knotty problems, he began to expand and enjoy himself.

He worked with Born on the application of quantum mechanics to the study of molecules and there was laid, following a paper reported in German, the basis for some or most of the conclusions reached at that date. Quantum is the Latin derivative of quantity. As used in physics it simply means a basic or elemental unit of energy. In perhaps simpler language, what Oppenheimer and Born did, after much scribbling and theorizing, was to work out the effect of energy on molecules and to fashion a kind of mathematical equation to prove their point. A molecule is the smallest particle of matter which has all the characteristics of the thing of which it is a part.

Within three weeks after Oppenheimer's arrival at the university, one of the loftiest institutions in the world, he was nominated for and awarded the degree of Doctor of Philosophy for the learned paper he wrote with Professor Born. In its presentation of the high degree, the university officials said they were proud that such a profound contribution to quantum mathematics had been made during the young man's student days.

Oppy left Göttingen and went on to Zurich in Switzerland where he spent a happy summer talking with Swiss mathematicians and elaborating on some of his abstruse theories. Between times he tried some mountain-climbing and did fairly well. Between times, too, he studied the history of Switzerland, went to see the magnificent structure housing the League of Nations, thought much of war and peace and was happier perhaps than he had ever been in his scholarly and introspective life.

From the University of Zurich he skipped to the University of Leiden in the Netherlands. For a week or two he strolled the streets carrying a glossary of terms, haunted the library of the university and spoke Dutch to everyone he met. To his astonishment he discovered that almost everyone he spoke with knew English, but he was determined to learn the Dutch language. Only six weeks after his arrival in Holland he delivered a lecture in almost impeccable Dutch to the student body and the faculty.

Now and then, stories about him began to drift back to scholastic circles. There were rumors, mainly unfounded, that he could read a printed page of complicated formulas and then recite them without fumbling. But his work done with Born at the University of Göttingen spread his reputation far and wide, for the paper was translated into many languages.

In short order, while at Leiden and while taking side trips to inspect the dikes in Holland, talking to the Dutch mathematicians, generally enjoying himself with long, solitary walks through the streets of lovely Amsterdam, he was offered professorships at the University of Berlin, at Leipsig and at the Sorbonne in Paris. These he turned down without much reflection. He wanted to go home and reassemble the startling theories he had chanced across in Europe concerning the composition of matter.

In late August of 1927 Oppenheimer set sail for the United States. He was now Dr. Oppenheimer; he had won the plaudits of many of the greatest physicists of Europe and he was tinkering idly in his own mind with the notion that if all the research about matter and energy were properly assembled, then an inexhaustible fund of energy—

through the splitting of the atom—could be achieved. The notion of an atomic bomb never crossed his mind. Immersed as he was in scholarly, academic circles, he had little contact with the ferocious and impending current events which were then churning up and which were to culminate in the greatest war in history.

In 1927, while Oppenheimer was in Germany, Switzerland and the Netherlands, there was in the shaping a grievous philosophy which declared that the strongest man or the strongest nation had the right to the best. The philosophy took on the name of fascism. One of the most curious aspects of this historical drift that might makes right was the idea that men of learning and vision were suspect and not to be trusted. Only men of muscle—gruff men, men who did not mind trespassing on the lands of others and who did not care about the hunger of others— were the best people in the world. These men were called the "strong men."

Curiously, while some sections of Europe, notably Germany and Italy, were busy trying to keep their thinkers from thinking and keeping their professors at the universities in line so that everyone would think the same way, men like Oppenheimer from the United States were thinking the way they wished. In many ways this thinking resulted in the defeat of the leaders of governments in Europe who were afraid of thought.

It is well worth mentioning that Oppy's experiences

in Europe, though short, were among the most stimulating of his life. What he heard and what he listened to and what new avenues of thought it gave him into the construction of matter and of higher mathematics, which would operate as the lever for the bursting open of the atom, were to prove of incalculable worth later on. In other words, he learned to think in a seasoned way for, after all, he had been consorting intellectually with some of the greatest minds in Europe. He also learned that many men were working in similar pathways but that there appeared to be no good clearing house of information in order to avoid duplication or, at worst, to effect co-operative effort.

During random talk he also wondered whether it were possible for men of great intellect ever to be free of economic want so that they could be free to serve science and mankind. All about him in Europe he saw great minds fettered to universities where they had to expend a good part of their energies and time in teaching rather than in the research they could do so well.

In 1928, while living with his parents again in New York City and still working on abstruse mathematical concepts, either alone or with one or another of the great American minds, he began to be troubled with a racking cough.

His cough grew worse to the point where his sleep was troubled and he began to lose weight steadily. Always a

very lean man, now he was gaunt. Finally he was persuaded to go to the Southwest for his doctors feared he
had contracted tuberculosis. It was hoped that in the dry,
invigorating air of the desert he would recover.

Oppenheimer was nothing loath. The idea of living in
the Southwest presented a good opportunity for peace
and a chance to continue his work. So with great joy and
a high sense of adventure, he went to Santa Fe, New
Mexico, not far from which he leased a primitive ranch.

The ranch didn't have many of the comforts of home
for the plumbing was poor or nonexistent and there was
neither electricity nor gas.

But Oppy happily had his books shipped out, bought
several fine saddle horses, put in a fine stock of German
wines, for which he had developed a taste abroad, and
resolved to have fun while losing his cough.

One of his first acts was the christening of his ranch
which he had refitted with some new furniture. Swinging
a bottle of kirschwasser, a German wine, he smashed it
against the hitching post and dubbed the house Perro
Caliente, or Hot Dog.

He bought himself a huge Stetson and with a light-
hearted feeling he packed a lunch of sandwiches or just
a bar of chocolate and headed for the Sangre de Cristo
Mountains. Sometimes he climbed them; other times he
just dabbled in his old sport of mineralogy.

Nights, he read by the light of an oil lamp and it must
have been a strange sight—this combination of primitive

ighting apparatus with the most advanced mathematic exts.

Sometimes he got bored and invented games. One day ie noted that the Mexican rug on his living room floor iear the fireplace had an intricate geometric pattern woven nto it. So he promptly proceeded to erect a geometric ame of tiddlywinks embracing equations and three dinensions.

It wasn't long before his cough began to leave him and iow and then he went to Sante Fe for X rays of his chest. He tried to eat properly and relaxed from his work by lipping into French poetry. He had a special fondness for Baudelaire.

Time slipped by dreamily and he learned to love the ast solitude about him and the homey people from near-by anches who often dropped by. If some of them thought iim strange because of his piles of books . . . well, it was he Southwest and what a man wanted to do to occupy is time was no one's business.

He began to put on a bit of weight though often he rode s far as fifty miles in one day. But so slender was he that ven the few pounds he added to his frame were noticeable. His skin developed a fine bronze and he began to look like rugged westerner.

He wrote to many of his new friends in Europe and he nade weekly treks to Sante Fe for his mail. Usually he had boxload of mineral specimens to send back to his rockoving friends in New York City. Undoubtedly the mail he received from his physicist friends in Europe was the most astonishing ever to cross the racks of the Sante F post office, filled as they were with intricate formulas and theories. Letters from Holland were especially amusing to him because his new friends addressed him as "Dear Opje," the Dutch translation of Oppy. He is still known today in Dutch circles of physicists as Opje.

In 1928 the world came knocking on his door. He was now well and for some time he had been thinking that i was time to leave his idyllic existence. He received several offers to teach, the most attractive among them being from the California Institute of Technology and the University of California. His work in Europe had attracted the atten tion of the heads of the departments and Oppy was torn between both offers.

At that time the West was the hub of the finest work being done in physics in the United States. It appeared as though the best men, attracted by the excellent opportunities and the well-endowed laboratories, were gravitating there. Oppy did not long remain torn between both offers. Impudently, he suggested to both universities that he could be useful to both at the same time.

While both universities were taken aback, after some reflection they saw nothing wrong with it and Oppy chuckled to his horse when he rode in for his mail and received the approvals: "Well, I guess a body can be in two places at the same time."

So Oppy joined with Cal Tech, as it is known, and with

the University of California—an association that was to last for twenty years and have a profound impact on thousands of students, on the universities themselves and on the youthful professor, now only twenty-four.

4

Man into Giant

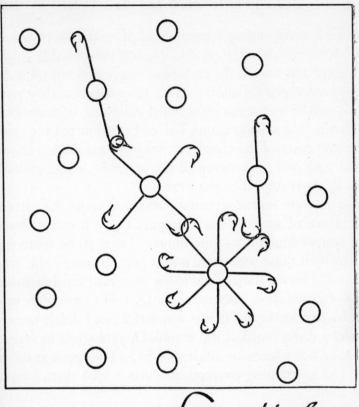

Lucretius

The faculty flocked to hear this incredible torrent of wit, amazed at his learning, his grasp of theory and mathematics. Students cut classes to come and sit in on Oppy's, and it was an amazing sight. The tall, lean, extremely handsome man with the bronzed skin appeared to be a never-ending fountainhead of quotes or equations from the minds of the world's greatest thinkers. He chain-smoked and flipped the stubs unerringly into ash trays; he gestured, raised his hands eloquently—and before they were lowered he was at the blackboard indicating with symbols what he was talking about. Before he completed the symbols he assumed the class knew what he was talking about, and with one wide sweep of the eraser he would embark on the next step, then the next.

This went on for several months, and under the careful guidance of some of his colleagues Oppy began to learn to temper himself, to tone himself down, to be more patient with those who were not as fast, to modify the brilliance of his vocabulary and to use more restrained rhetoric. As one professor, Richard Tolman, told Oppy after one of his first lectures: "It was wonderful but I didn't understand a damn word of it." It took Oppy a while to realize that he was addressing students who had not gone as far as he had in grasping concepts and that it took them longer to learn.

There was one period during his early months of teaching when he was sure he was being understood and that the students were drinking in what he was saying with avid interest. Then he was tipped off. It seemed that so cadenced was the flow of his voice and so beautiful his choice of phraseology, that his listeners were being almost hypnotized—not by what he was saying but by how he was saying it.

When he ceased being a legend because he was too far advanced and became one because a class with him was a stimulating, never-to-be-forgotten thing, his students would accompany him from Berkeley for the Cal Tech term. En route they would have roadside seminars. His own rooms were always jammed with students eating, arguing, shouting, appealing to him. So youthful looking was he then, as he is today, that one could not have distinguished him from his students.

All across the country and at the universities of many nations abroad, the physics staffs are full of Oppy's "boys." Physics and theory of physics, as we know it today, was practically in its infancy just those very short years ago when Oppy began to teach and delve at the California universities.

As he began to clarify his teaching methods, he found that his classroom work became less exhausting. He began horseback riding again on the lovely paths about Berkeley and he even danced a bit. He also amused himself by taking up Sanskrit. He made friends with the great Sanskrit expert Arthur Ryder, and every Thursday evening he attended a reading of the great Hindu poets. His friendships widened and soon included philosophers on the staff of the university—poets, writers, geologists, engineers, lawyers and physicians.

He found a fine affinity among all the specialties, which was to stand him in good stead later on when he was to take over the directorship of the Institute for Advanced

Study. For there is a kinship among all scholarly pursuits and there is a great and understanding kinship among scholars, no matter what their fields. The poet and the scientist work the same way and seek the same things. Just beneath the surface of the poet's longing to express an idea is the idea itself. And this also holds true of the scientist. It is in the seeking and in the agony and joy of seeking that the poet and the scientist have this kinship.

In a short time Oppy's friends began to include people of various shades of opinion, of color, of nativity and of scope. As he talked, he learned. Always a good talker, he inspired others to talk well. He plunged into Oriental philosophies, poetry, the strange and daring theories of the physicists then on the West Coast, art, music, economics, architecture, even furnishings. He literally seethed through a day. The word boredom had no meaning for him. All about him were people teeming with ideas he had always thought possible and he responded to them with the eagerness of a discoverer. All about him, too, he heard people expound ideas he had never thought about. And here, too, he responded with an agility that pleased his friends, for no one is so much flattered as when his own ideas are elaborated upon.

His own rooms became too crowded for the multitudes of people who crowded into them to argue, to shout, to engage in rococo argument. He moved to a house on the side of a canyon on Shasta Road and still continued to be the student—to listen, to learn, to argue, to harangue, to confound and then perhaps to admit himself beaten. In other words, Oppy developed to the titan he is today by remaining the student while he was the teacher.

As Oppy's intellectual life expanded, so did his personal one. He met lovely, vivacious, dark-haired Katherine Puening Harrison, who was doing postgraduate work in mycology at the University of California, Los Angeles, and after a whirlwind courtship, unlike most stories of the careful professor, they were married.

After much talk they decided to stay in California. For one thing, Oppy liked his posts at Cal Tech and the University of California. For another, everything that Oppy dreamed about for the future was taking place in California. The most advanced work in the experimental branches of physics was going forward at a rapid pace. And later on, it was to prove to be a good thing.

There, for example, was E. O. Lawrence building his first cyclotron and laying down the blueprints of the ten-thousand-ton giants to come. There was Carl Anderson of Cal Tech, a good friend of Oppy's, who was pushing forward with uncanny prescience the cosmic ray research begun by Robert A. Millikan, the great genius. Not many yards away, there was still another wonderful madman who was planning a two-hundred-inch telescope mirror which was to be accurate to the fraction of a second of an arc. Oppy felt that he was in the midst of great impending events. All about him at the California universities and laboratories there were men who were seeking to probe beneath still another layer of the unknown. Perhaps, he felt, it was part of the adventurous spirit of the great open spaces where no holds were barred, where scientific inhibitions were fewer than he had found elsewhere.

While he had developed and had been greatly influenced in Europe, there still was a feeling there that a formula laid down by a famous dead man had to be followed in its entirety, otherwise it was heresy.

Here in California, where physics appeared to have arrived at an easy, searching, expanding elasticity, nothing was sacred except the next truth.

On the other hand, Oppy was urged to stay in California. Many of his colleagues and the university officials told him that his headlong drive, his enthusiasm, his forward ideas— these were essential to the growth not only of the new physics but the new forces which the new physics promised to unleash.

His reputation was extraordinary in that his name was not especially identified with any single bit of research or any particular achievement—and yet he was famous. It is all the more to his credit that it was his vast range of scholarship in so many fields and the love his students and colleagues bore for him that he was persuaded to stay on.

Though his name has never been latched onto a particular bit of research, his published theories on certain aspects of theoretical physics won for him, in the opinion of many scientists, a top ranking among the ten greatest theoretical physicists in the world.

His interests and personal research, for example, took him through the gamut of modern physics to relativistic wave mechanics and quantum electrodynamics to astrophysics and cosmic rays. His steadiest interest was focused upon the elementary particles, the ultimate building blocks of the physical world. In a sense, he is the godfather of the two newest and perhaps most elusive particles, the meson and the positron.

At that time his work on the positron was overshadowed by two Nobel prize winners—Dirac, who was later to come to the Institute, and Carl D. Anderson, a colleague at Cal Tech.

Dirac, who was severely criticized by Oppy on a theory pertaining to the positron, accepted the Oppenheimer finding and accordingly revised his theory. Anderson, as well, revised his idea and also gave Oppenheimer full credit when he found in laboratory tests that Oppy's paper work had been accurate.

Later on, Oppy fulfilled the theories of a Japanese scientist named Hideki Yukawa and Anderson by actually bridging the gap between the theory and the discovery of the particle called the meson.

Oppy's studies in cosmic rays gave him the assurance of the existence of the meson and a few months later Anderson caught the track of the meson on a photographic plate, confirming Oppenheimer's theory and proof.

Another piece of research that won for Oppenheimer an immortality among scientists was the explanation of a phenomenon known as the Oppenheimer-Phillips Effect.

In conjunction with Melba Phillips, another physicist, Oppenheimer was able to show that a baffling movement of a deuteron (heavy hydrogen nucleuses), being loosely bound, surrenders its neutron on entering the field of a heavy nucleus. The Effect, as it is known, showed that the heavy nucleus captures the stripped neutron, becomes unstable and radioactive. Then the remainder of the deuteron, being just a proton freed from its abnormal bond, survives as a nucleus of ordinary hydrogen.

While all this may be complex at this point, suffice it to say that Oppenheimer's researches have a great deal to do with the development of what is known as the hydrogen bomb, the city destroyer, the force millions of times more potent than the atomic bomb—an explanation of which will be found in a later chapter.

With marriage, of course, the program of his days took on more healthful shapes and meanings. Kitty would no longer permit him the exacting luxury of talking half the night and then reading until dawn. He was reminded to eat on time and at regular intervals, and when a cold or some other disturbance would strike him, a doctor would be called.

Those were the quiet years in California—the sedate but exciting ones. They were the days when physics was being stood on its head by Oppy, his colleagues about him and physicists across the world. Curiously, the public was completely unaware of the fast-rushing events in science taking place at the universities—especially in California—that appeared to coincide with the fast-rushing events that were taking place in Nazi Germany.

The Oppenhemers' lovely home on Eagle Hill with a magnificent view of the famous Golden Gate was soon filled to overflowing with exquisite art treasures—many of them originals which Kitty or Oppy couldn't resist buying, though the prices of such masterpieces were high. Not that they bought only the works of the established artists. Sometimes the work of an unknown would come their way and, fascinated by brush technique or theme or bold design, they would buy that, too.

Soon the handsome home began to resemble a museum and the Oppenheimers with great reluctance surrendered some of their prizes to a San Francisco art museum.

It was difficult for Kitty to believe that her handsome, learned and popular husband had been a "bookworm," a dull stick, not many years previously. She did not believe this until one day Oppy came across his yearbook for 1926 from Harvard University. Beneath the photos of every graduate was of course a list of the clubs they belonged to, the teams they were on, the university newspapers and magazines they had been on, the class positions they held.

But under Oppy's name there was just the scant and bleak phrase: "In college three years as an undergraduate." That's all.

Meanwhile, his brother Frank, with whom Oppy had maintained a steady and affectionate correspondence through the years, was developing into an important man of parts, much to the pleasure and excitement of his parents.

In 1933 Frank obtained his bachelor's degree in science from the famed Johns Hopkins University and then spent two years at Cambridge.

Poppa Oppenheimer then sent Frank off to Europe where he spent a year at the University of Florence in Italy. He then went on to California, where he and Oppy measured each other as brothers and friends and won a new and proud recognition of each other. These were good days for both, seeing each other expand into men of science and stature.

In 1939 Frank won his degree of Doctor of Philosophy in physics at the California Institute of Technology and of course Oppy was at the commencement exercises. That same year Oppy was a reference for his brother who was appointed a physicist at Stanford University. No one was prouder than big brother.

In 1941 Mrs. Oppenheimer gave birth to Peter and a new and important element entered the household. Oppy immediately began to devour books on bringing up children and on pediatrics. Like any father, however, he jumped with alarm at an untoward cry.

The events which were to catapult Oppenheimer into world-wide fame were then driving forward with relentless fury. Already known to physicists and scholars the world over, he was to become a household name to the people.

In 1938, after several years of trying to placate Adolf Hitler, Fuehrer of the German people, the British Empire was forced to declare war when the Nazis showed that no amount of appeasement would stay them from their lunge to world conquest.

While the United States was not yet involved, there were rumbles in the Far Pacific, where Japan, goaded by her treaty partner Germany, was making threatening movements. The sympathies of the people of the United States were with England, France and the small countries which had been overrun and enslaved by the Nazi bully. Too, stories of atrocities in concentration camps against minorities or against those who did not subscribe to the Nazi movement shocked and horrified the American people. Meantime, President Franklin D. Roosevelt began to render as much aid as he could to the Western Allies without endangering the position of the United States.

But it was not enough. France, weakened by traitors within and overwhelmed by a highly mechanized German army, was soon overwhelmed by superior forces, better-trained troops and a mighty German air armada. Soon the Netherlands, one of Oppy's favorite nations, was overcome and the German Air Force, to "teach the people of Europe a lesson," willfully bombed and destroyed a good section of undefended Rotterdam.

At highly placed councils in Washington it was soon

recognized that science, as never before, would play the mightiest role in the war of aggression by the German Nazis who had been joined in their assaults by Fascist Italy.

Soon there began to be established a kind of loose liaison between men of science teaching at universities in the United States or working on the staffs of great manufacturers and government officials. Soon, too, high officers of the United States Army, the Navy and the Air Force found themselves consulting with men of science. These military men began to pick up the terminologies used in science and began to feel more and more that without new and more efficient weapons the aggressors would overrun the earth.

At that time, too, Germany had a very high degree of scientific stature. Her men of science were ranked among the world's best and it soon appeared that the brains of the democratic nations would be pitted against those of the totalitarian countries where dictators ran the seats of governments.

Feverishly, there began to be set up all sorts of scientific boards which would advise the United States military. This reached new highs of concentration when Hitler repeatedly kept boasting that he had new, secret weapons which would win the war overnight.

Some scientists guessed that Hitler was boasting of a new poison gas or perhaps of microbe warfare which would kill off cattle and people when sprayed from planes. But the physicists in the United States and in Britain felt that Hitler meant just one thing: to use a bomb of colossal power, made possible by the splitting of the atom, and which would have the smash of leveling a city in a twinkling.

Japanese scientists, as well, were working feverishly to help their country in a war in which they were sure Japan would be involved.

Japan struck with fury and without warning on December 7, 1941, at Pearl Harbor, killing thousands and gutting a good section of the United States Pacific Fleet. America was immediately involved in the war and the tension was especially felt on the West Coast where there were rumors of an impending invasion by Japanese troops.

Feeling ran high, political differences were dropped and the nation girded for war. But it was terribly unprepared simply because it had not been setting up the vast factories so essential to modern warfare matériel. Time was of the essence if the Nazis, the Fascists and the Japanese were to be kept from producing first a dread weapon of such caliber as to render an opposing nation impotent and crushed in a short time.

The high officials of the United States knew that if the enemy were to develop such a dread weapon, it would use it without mercy and without hesitation.

California, the center of high-level theoretical physics, had of course been engrossed for many years with the mysteries of nuclear fission, and Oppenheimer was no exception.

As is true of all scientific triumphs, a great deal of work and theorizing over long, long periods had gone into the thinking about the atomic structure of matter. When the culmination came, it was as much a matter of organization and disciplined thinking as genius.

Late in 1942, while there were some encouraging signs, such as the successful invasion of North Africa by the huge United States fleet which later furnished a springboard to the continent of Europe, things were not going well for the Allies. Hitler's hand stretched across Europe and clutched it like a mighty mailed gantlet. In the Pacific the Japanese had taken vast territories, were threatening Australia and as yet were not greatly opposed by the growing United States naval strength.

Meanwhile, unknown to the public and unknown to all but the very highest officials such as President Roosevelt, Winston Churchill, prime minister of Great Britain, J. Edgar Hoover, director of the Federal Bureau of Investigation, Army, Navy, Air Force Chiefs of Staff and a few others, there was shaping up the most secret and most significant project in the history of man: The splitting of the atom.

It all began with Albert Einstein, the celebrated physicist. On August 2, 1939, Einstein sent a letter to President Roosevelt in which he stressed the need for a government-sponsored project in atomic energy. In his letter he underscored the researches that had been effected in Nazi Germany and he warned that if the United States did not subsidize such a defense fund to look into the possibilities of splitting the atom, the potential enemy would control the world through force and devastation.

President Roosevelt responded immediately by setting up a committee on atomic energy. The committee convened on October 21, 1939, and made several recommendations. The response came in the form of a fund of six thousand dollars, a laughable sum in view of what was to be spent later on.

In 1940 Einstein again wrote to Roosevelt and gave implicit warning that the Nazis were coming closer to splitting the atom and he urged that the commission be given unlimited funds with which to hire the best scientists, both American and European, and to push forward research and experimentation so that the atom could be split, a devastating bomb made and the war ended as speedily as possible with a minimum loss of life.

"Otherwise," Einstein's letter said, "there is a great chance that the Germans will be the first to seize the advantage and will use the atomic bomb ruthlessly to destroy all free peoples who stand in their way."

Shortly afterwards Roosevelt appropriated monies from a secret war fund which he had available to use in contingencies pertaining to national security. He then ordered the harnessing of the nation's best brains in the race for the atomic bomb.

In the fall of 1942 Oppenheimer was awakened in the middle of the night by the ringing of the telephone.

"This is Major General Leslie R. Groves. I have just flown in from Washington and I must see you immediately."

Sitting in his living room in just his robe, Oppenheimer was informed by General Groves that he had been selected to head up the top secret atomic bomb project which was to change the history of mankind.

"Excuse me while I change my clothes," Oppy said. "And I must inform my wife."

"You tell nothing to no one," said the general. And that's how it was for a long time to come.

It was no accident that Oppy was selected. It was on the advice of the best minds in America.

5

In the Beginning . . .

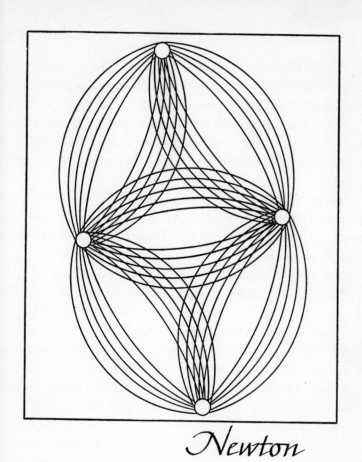

Newton

More than two thousand years ago, men began to question the things they saw about them. As they quested, they tried to break down into component parts all the matter with which they came into contact. As a start, they broke these things down into four components: Fire, water, earth and air. They called these things elements and they were sure that everything contained all or some of these elements.

Some wise men believed that all things on earth contained all of these four ingredients; some thought that these ingredients could be broken down into still smaller parts.

There was, for example, a man called Democritus, a Greek who lived in the Golden Age of thought, who said that everything was made up of particles of matter which could not be seen.

A man who opposed his theory waved a lump of gold in his face and said: "Look! Here is a lump of gold. Do you mean to tell me that this is not all of one piece?"

"No," shouted Democritus. "I see it is hard to the touch. I can feel it is hard to the touch. But I feel strongly that it is made up of tiny particles we cannot see or feel."

While Democritus was hooted, many young, serious students gathered about him and urged him to tell them more if he could.

"I think the whole world is made up of things I like to call 'building blocks,' the kind of things children play with," Democritus said. Even at that time children played with cubes of wood with which they constructed temples and homes.

"I will call these building blocks 'atoms' because the building blocks with which children play are sections, and we call them *atomos*," Democritus said.

This idea grew until a man named Aristotle came along. He postulated the notion about fire, water, earth and air and this theory stuck for a long, long time. He called all matter basic elements of the four ingredients.

Aristotle made a lot of trouble for as men continued to think, they got the idea that if certain formulas could be arrived at, the elements of one thing could be changed into another. They thought, for example, that if enough work could be put into dross metals such as iron, the basic elements would change and the cheap metal would be transformed into gold, the precious metal.

For more than a thousand years emperors and kings hired men to try and change one metal into another, preferably gold. These men failed, often incurring the anger of their masters. Many had their heads chopped off because they failed to achieve the impossible by stirring all kinds of boiling mixtures. They were on the right track but long years away from a true concept.

The boiling and mixing and chopping off of heads went on for quite a while until John Dalton, a British Quaker, physicist and schoolteacher, said that gold could not be made of other matter because the atoms of one element are different from another.

"The alchemists," he said in 1808, "have not recognized the problem with which they were coping. Gold is an element and the atoms of each element are so different from each other that it would take a miracle to make gold from dross metal."

During the latter half of the nineteenth century, however, men began to think even more deeply. They came to a recognition that the atom, as propounded by the ancients, was not the smallest bit of matter at all. They began to feel very sure that there were even smaller things within the atom.

The scientists of the last century came up with the notion that perhaps all the parts of an atom were held together by something called "electrical abstraction."

Though these scientists did not know exactly what they meant by "electrical abstraction," they did go on to say that there must be spaces between the parts inside of an atom.

They felt that the atom was a very small thing but that the things which composed an atom were even smaller. Curiously, such was the wonderful thinking done during the last century—without the aid of excellent instruments or any instruments of any consequence—that much of what was thought has come to pass as being true and valid.

For example, it is known today that if you spent your time for a full year counting atoms, you would not arrive at enough to cover the head of a pin even if you counted day and night without sleeping.

Roughly, it is estimated that about thirty-six billion atoms can sit comfortably on the head of a pin. In numerals this would read like this: 36,000,000,000.

Now within the atom there are nuclei, infinitesimal particles, which total about one million multiplied by million. In other words—or rather numerals—the number of nuclei in an atom would read like this: 1,000,000,-000,000,000,000.

So, the number of nuclei that could sit on the head of a pin, in round numbers, looks something like this: 36,000,-000,000,000,000,000,000,000,000.

That's an awful lot of particles of matter to sit on the head of a pin. But that's how it is and that's how matter is constituted.

Because these nuclei are so tiny it is a great tribute to them that they are so important to energy. After all, we burn so many tons of coal to make so much electrical energy. We burn so many hundreds of gallons of gas to fly such and such a plane. How is it that within the precincts of an atom, containing so many astronomical neutrons, there is so much awaiting man's pleasure?

About the best way of imagining the size of a neutron is to imagine a grapefruit against the size of the state of Texas. It must be remembered that Texas is not only the biggest state in the union but bigger than France and Belgium combined. Thus, the size of the grapefruit, as compared with the geographical expanse, is not very large.

In 1896 Professor Antoine Henri Becquerel found that some elements change by themselves. By this time it had been found that the world was not composed of four elements alone but of ninety-two. These ninety-two elements were numbered according to their protons, the "plus" electrical charges emanating from an atom.

Professor Becquerel, toying with uranium, found that it gave off rays and was "transforming" itself, as he called it. An assistant of his, Marie Curie, begged her master to allow her to experiment. Between them they discovered that some elements are radioactive and that they give off "protons," or plus charges. Later, from Madame Curie' strange experiments, there developed radium which gave life-healing qualities while she herself was to die of it death-dealing qualities absorbed during her work with the new, weird, "alive" element.

In 1919 Sir Ernest Rutherford, a British physicist, discovered that he could use radioactive elements to bombard other elements. "I use the rays as bullets," he explained

With these rays Sir Ernest was able to "plaster" a nucleus of nitrogen with radium rays and transform it into oxygen This was the first instance of alchemy come to success and the first artificial transmutation of elements.

It was not much later on that men were building cyclotrons, machines which whirled at high speeds and which imparted high speeds at the same time to electrified particle which bombarded nucleuses of atoms. In many instance these took the place of such radioactive elements of radium which were expensive and could not quite be applied fo experimental bombardments of the nucleuses of atoms o other elements.

It was a beginning—and a long way from the early Greeks who had postulated the notion of the atom.

Scientists of the early part of the twentieth century ha

gone quite a long way since the ancients, but except for the newer and revolutionary theories, very little actual work, from a physical standpoint, had been done to prove or disprove old Democritus. He was righter than he thought.

6

What was Known, What was to be Done

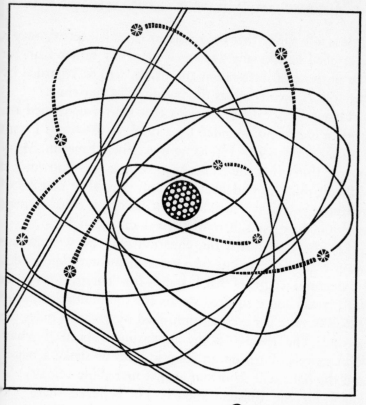

Uranium

tomic energy was heralded into the world with such
explosive drama that the news of it has been voted
by ranking newspapermen of all nations as the most
important story of the half century, overshadowing even
the cataclysmic events of both world wars.

It is safe to say that the release of atomic energy, once it is applied beneficially (as surely it must) rather than for the purpose of devastation and death, will be regarded by the historian to come as the big news of our time.

Generally speaking, the idea that matter contained energy was first propounded by a clerk in the Swiss Patent Office back in 1905. His name was Albert Einstein. Many people think that the Einstein theory, as it is known, is a difficult thing to understand. Simply put, all it consists of is a little equation which says that energy is equal to mass multiplied by the square of the velocity of light.

On the blackboard the equation may be written this way: $E = mc^2$. Anyone who has an elementary knowledge of algebra recognizes that E stands for "energy," m stands for "mass" and c squared stands for the multiplication of 186,300 miles per second multiplied by 186,300 miles per second. The 186,300 is the approximate speed at which light travels. Turn on an electric bulb or strike a match and the light will shoot out at that incredible velocity. So much for the Einstein theory. He believed there was energy locked up in the atom and he has since been confirmed in his belief with staggering results.

The Belgian Congo contains rich stores of a pitchblende ore containing uranium, an element at one time used mainly as a source of radium and as a pigment by people who make paints and ceramics. No one paid much attention to the uranium riches to be found in this primitive part o he world until some busybodies working in laboratories, devoured with curiosity, began to bombard it, to subject t to rays or particles which penetrated it!

In England in 1932 Sir James Chadwick, a physicist, was putting pellets of radium, the size of ball bearings in kates, inside of balls of the rare, metallic element called beryllium—the size perhaps of a small potato or onion. Sir ames found, to his excitement, that rays from the radium icked out neutrons from the beryllium.

Neutrons—and the word comes from neuter or neutral —have neither a positive nor a negative charge. In other words, they are uncharged. Because they are uncharged, hey are able to penetrate nuclei.

The nucleus in physics means simply the central part r core of the atom. It contains most of the mass of the tom and has a positive charge equal to the atomic number f the element of which it is a component. If this is difficult, think of the nuclei as simply the core in a tennis ball r a golf ball.

Chadwick's experiment, besides kicking out neutrons, lso kicked up great excitement elsewhere in the world. n Italy, for instance, a dark, balding physicist named Enco Fermi won a Nobel prize in 1938 for what he did to ollow up on Sir James.

Before turning to Fermi, a great friend and admirer of Oppenheimer's, it is necessary to point out that those neuons knocked out by Sir James were highly dangerous to people. The combination of radium and beryllium had to be encased in lead for the rays could be deadly or at best very harmful.

What Fermi did was to set up the very same experiment but he used the neutrons which were kicked out as bombs on all kinds of substances. What he was after was to find out if the bombarding neutrons would "stick" to the atoms of the substances under fire and turn out entirely new atoms.

Fermi, a highly imaginative man, used one substance after another. He did not let up but shot his neutrons into many elements. This went on for quite a while. Finally one day Fermi discovered what he thought to be new atoms. He was able to determine this by using a Geiger counter which detects radioactivity. His new atoms, which were isotopes of the original atom, were radioactive and he was highly pleased.

One day, in 1934, Fermi subjected uranium to bombardment. Uranium, which is Element 92 in the periodic table, is not only the heaviest of all the elements but highly complex. When the neutrons assailed the uranium the victim not only became radioactive but gave off four different radioactive emanations.

Fermi sat down and pondered this. He could only reason that he had discovered four new heavier-than-uranium elements. It was a reasonable assumption simply because the tiny nuclear particles were now much heavier than Element

92—uranium. They had actually converted themselves into another form of matter.

The stir in the scientific world was tremendous. Except for a few sparse items in the press, this notable event went unmarked by the general public. Even if the news had hit the headlines of the world press, the chances are that readers would not have become very excited about the news because the difficulties of rendering such complex experiments into simple language would have been, at the time, perhaps impossible. Since then, of course, newspapermen and the public have become familiar to some degree with the language and the implications of new developments.

However, scientists all over the world were much interested. In France many physicists rushed to bombard uranium and confirmed Fermi's findings. It looked as though the periodic table, which had stood up for quite a while, was due for a change.

In Germany, where scientists of the period were going through trying times because of the Hitler dictatorship and strange and bestial laws regarding race, Fermi's experiments were also repeated and there were sudden demands upon suppliers for uranium specimens.

In the fall of 1938 there appeared a sensational article in an academic magazine called *Die Naturwissenschaften*. Written by two German physicists F. Strassmann and O. Hahn, the article said that while repeating Fermi's experimental bombardment on uranium, they had thought they would find four new elements, heavier than uranium and of course bearing the numbers, 93, 94, 95 and 96. To their amazement, they said, after scrutinizing what had come up they had found that one of the four new, converted elements was nothing more or less than barium, one of the middleweight elements tagged as No. 56 on the periodic table. They confessed that they were baffled but they also said that their findings knocked all theories of nuclear physics right on its head.

"What has happened shows that there is a tremendous contradiction someplace," they wrote. "We cannot be wrong," they said with stunning German logic. While they were not wrong, they were too close to what they had discovered to see the value of what they had found.

The article was read in Copenhagen by a brilliant scientist named Lise Meitner. Of Jewish extraction, Lise Meitner had left Germany to avoid persecution. It is wonderful to speculate that Hitler actually destroyed himself and lost the war because he pushed forward anti-Semitic laws. Had Lise Meitner still been working with Strassmann at the Kaiser-Wilhelm Institute in Berlin, she, as a scientist, would have come to the same conclusions as she did in Copenhagen, Hitler would have had the atomic bomb, would have used it without mercy and would have won the war and perhaps the world. Fortunately, however, things turned out otherwise, and what took place in Copenhagen showed vividly the geographical spread of the development of atomic fission from England to the Congo to Italy to France to Germany and to Denmark.

Working with her nephew O. R. Frisch at the University of Copenhagen, Dr. Meitner duplicated the experiments of Strassmann and Hahn and came up with a daring hypothesis to explain what the Germans had perhaps overlooked.

This explanation, which was sent to the British publication *Nature*, suggested that perhaps the nucleus of uranium was actually composed of particles which acted like a drop of liquid. When the drop was disturbed it got into tremendous motion. They then went on to say:

"If the movement is made sufficiently violent by adding energy, such a drop may divide itself into two smaller drops.

"It seems therefore possible that the uranium nucleus has only a small stability of form, and may, after neutron capture, divide itself into two nuclei of roughly equal size."

The two scientists named this process fission!

Strassmann and Hahn, without knowing it, had actually split the atom, the uranium atom!

Now why does the splitting of the uranium atom release energy? The answer is simple.

When an atom is split—very much like a piece of kindling wood is split with an ax—it divides into two parts. The combined weight of the two pieces of wood would equal the weight of the wood before it was split. But when scientists weighed the two parts of the atom they found that the two weighed somewhat *less* than the atom had weighed in the first place.

What was lost was matter being converted into energy. It just went away; it was just converted into energy. Remember what we said about the Einstein theory, about matter being composed of energy?

Another good question at this stage would be to ask why only uranium undergoes fission. Why not other elements? Well, other elements do fission. For example, when thorium (No. 90 on the periodic table) is bombarded it also fissions. But uranium behaves better, for practical purposes, than any of the others. For the atomic structure of uranium, when bombarded with neutrons of very low energy or even by just one lonely single neutron, is set into frightful motion and splits easily.

And the most logical question which should be asked at this time is: What is atomic energy and what takes place when a neutron invades the precincts of uranium atoms?

Here is the answer: The neutron is gulped in by the very heavy nucleus of uranium. The very center of the uranium atom agitates violently. It begins to quiver like a drop of water hanging at the end of a medicine dropper. The drop becomes longer and longer and now assumes the shape of a pulled-out dumbbell. Longer and longer becomes the drop as it vibrates—then presto! the two fat parts of the dumbbell fall apart, or rather fly apart. This is fission.

WHAT WAS KNOWN, WHAT WAS TO BE DONE

All right. They scud with frightful speed away from each other—faster than anything you can think of except light. The speed is estimated at ten thousand miles per second, if you can imagine a speed like that.

How far do they go? Perhaps no farther than an inch or so in the air. If the fission takes place within solid uranium, the two particles may go only about one thousandth of an inch.

But while this flying apart at tremendous speed is on, a vast heat is set up which is atomic energy. Simple? The split atom sections give a fantastic amount of energy to neighboring atoms—and that's all there is to it.

It's well worth mentioning that Frisch, continuing on by himself, checked and rechecked the assumptions made by him and Dr. Meitner and found that he was correct. It was fission; the atom had been split, just as it has been described above.

Dr. Niels Bohr, the great Danish physicist, was given an advance copy of the Meitner-Frisch findings and brought the news to the United States. This was in January, 1939.

Physicists were almost crazy with excitement. Had it been anyone of less stature than Bohr, perhaps they would not have believed that the atom had been split. Until then, outside scientific circles the splitting of the atom was a kind of theme for cartoonists or vaudevillians.

Just about that time Dr. Fermi arrived to take over a post at Columbia University. When he was told the great news he immediately set to work. Other scientists also began to make their own feverish experiments and the press, in effect, missed the big news by just running a short item here or there. The New York *Times*, for example, carried a short item buried in the back pages saying only that Dr. Bohr had declared "that bombardment of a small amount of pure isotope 235 of uranium with slow neutrons would start a 'chain reaction' or atomic explosion sufficiently great to blow up a laboratory and the surrounding country for many miles." Bohr, by the way, was to come back to the United States after escaping from the Nazi invaders and help to work on the Big Firecracker under Oppenheimer.

Since up above we used the new and now familiar word isotope, it may be best to explain what it means. Some elements—for example, gold—contain atoms which have equal weight. One atom in gold will weigh exactly as much as another. But other elements have atoms of different weights. These are called isotopes. In other words, an isotope is a form of the element in every respect except atomic weight.

It is now interesting to go back to a wonderful experiment that took place in 1935 at the University of Chicago. A scientist named Dr. Arthur J. Dempster was working on the component parts of elements with a weird machine he himself had designed. This machine could tell the weights of the atoms of any of the elements.

Well, one day Dr. Dempster brought his machine to bear on uranium. It had always been taken for granted that uranium had one single isotope. It bore the label U-238, meaning uranium, of course, with the 238 standing for the total weight of the atoms.

To his amazement his machine, which is very complex to describe, caught the fact on a photographic plate that uranium had an isotope which came under the weight number of 235. This kicked up no great fuss in scientific circles because, as we have mentioned, uranium was not a big hero at the time.

But later experiments in 1940 at Columbia University showed that it was this elusive fellow, U-235 and not U-238, which was fissioning under the impact of slow neutrons.

Now that fission was an accomplished and understood process, what was the gigantic task confronting Oppenheimer and his staff?

Simply this. Splitting an atom makes a little fuss, a small explosion hardly worth anyone's notice. The thing was to get a big hunk of uranium to explode. How to get all the atoms to blow up in a chain reaction, that was the poser.

Again, Dr. Fermi comes into the picture. He theorized that if one neutron could kick up great excitement in an atom and thereby cause other neutrons to be released, then the "made" neutrons could be put to work to create more atom-splitting and so on into a colossal bang. This is called chain reaction, a very lucid phrase.

Armed with this theory, Dr. Fermi arranged to talk to a group of Washington military men and convince them of the fact that there was a good possibility of developing a superbomb. They listened to him but were unimpressed.

As we know, however, Einstein did send off that letter in August of 1939 and a pittance was appropriated. Meanwhile, the British were quick to recognize the potentials in U-235 and under the leadership of Sir James Chadwick were forging ahead rapidly in their research.

By the middle of 1941 Sir James in a report told the British government: "We are satisfied that the project of making an atomic bomb is practicable and likely to lead to decisive results in the war."

Intelligence services in the United States and advisers from the British government warned repeatedly that the Nazis were working day and night on the making of an atomic bomb. Winston Churchill, prime minister of England, had a long conference on this with President Roosevelt and soon the United States began to wake up.

On December 6, 1941, just a day before Pearl Harbor, it was announced that the race for the atomic bomb was now a major effort sponsored by the United States government.

The race was now on for the Big Bomb—and for all mankind.

7.

"We Shook the Tree of Knowledge . . ."

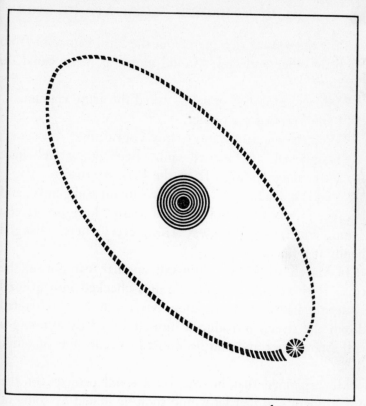

Hydrogen

O ne fall day in 1942, *not long after a tall, angular man* accompanied by a stocky one had been seen prowling about the neighborhood, an army jeep rolled up to a camp set on a mesa called Los Alamos, somewhat west of Santa Fe. The owner of the camp, which was a "dude" run for the sons of rich men from the East, came out from his little office and said: "Good morning, what can I do for you?"

"You're Frank O'Connell?" asked the army captain.

"I am," replied the owner.

"Well, Uncle Sam wants to buy your camp."

"Won't sell," O'Connell said. "Been doing well here for years since I retired from the Park Service."

"You'll sell, all right," the army captain said gently, and because it was for Uncle Sam, it wasn't long before the camp, which was far away from everywhere, changed hands at a fair price.

In March of 1943 the same tall, angular man got off the train at the depot in Santa Fe and checked into a hotel under the name of Mr. Bradley. After a shower he strolled down the street, introduced himself to a lady running a real estate office and said he wanted to rent "lots of office room."

He explained that he was on a small project for the government and that he would soon be joined by some of his co-workers who would need desk room. The lady was delighted and leased him five offices all around a patio at 109 East Palace Street.

In a few days the trains stopping at Santa Fe continued to drop off quiet-spoken men who didn't much bother to glance at the menus in the restaurants when they dined and who didn't seem to care for the pleasures that the town had to offer. Their names were as innocuous as that of

Mr. Bradley. One called himself Baker; another Farmer; another said he went by the handle of Smith. It seemed that representatives of the most popular names in America were meeting in convention at Santa Fe.

It was soon apparent to Mr. Bradley that he needed a secretary and several sharp-featured gentlemen immediately went to work on the past histories of several likely young ladies who were looking for work. They finally boiled the applicants down to an intelligent girl called Dottie who immediately wanted to know what kind of work she was going to do. "Secretarial," was the laconic answer.

She met her new boss and liked him and his smile immediately. The first few days it was difficult for her to tell just what her duties were to be. It seemed that strangers were constantly arriving and it was her job to find beds and meals for them and to arrange, as best she might, some means of getting them to the mesa, which was now ringed by guards for miles about.

The townsfolk didn't know what to make of all this but the strangers made no trouble and seemed very absent-minded. One local wit named Mr. Bradley's project: "Army Submarine Base." That was a good joke for a while. Then somebody else thought of "Project Wind-shield Wiper"—and that's what it became.

It wasn't long, of course, before Dottie discovered that Mr. Baker was the world-famous scientist Niels Bohr, while Farmer was the renowned Italian physicist Fermi, and that her immediate boss was the celebrated J. Robert Oppenheimer. Otherwise, she knew nothing about the project itself.

Beneath the casual air presented to the townsfolk there was feverish activity. Tons of material began pouring in, houses went up, wives and children (including Kitty and Peter) arrived and the new town on the mesa began to take on the appearance of a full-fledged hamlet where not too long ago there had been nothing but the shacks of the "dude" ranch.

Various intelligence services set up headquarters for miles about and the personnel was checked and rechecked. The magnificent part of the whole operation—and Oppenheimer controlled it utterly and completely—was that when the work was done, when the thunder had been drawn from the sun, no one knew what had been going on except those who were told about it. Despite rumors of so-called "leaks," the fact of the matter is that no enemy and no friendly nation received any so-called secrets about the atomic bomb. Oppenheimer is particularly sensitive about the phrase "atomic secrets." There are none, he maintains. It's all a matter of engineering.

Within a few months after the plant was going full blast, the strain began to tell on Oppenheimer and his chief assistants. His weight dropped to a low of one hundred and fifteen pounds; he rarely saw Kitty and came home only to take a bath. As director of the project, the Oppenheimers had the right to occupy one of the houses on what came to be called "Bathtub Row." It was named that simply because there were a few houses on the street which actually possessed a tub. There had been no provisions made for comfort; there was no time and no one cared.

Oppy was virtually the mayor of the town which in two, frenzied, hectic years grew to a population of forty-five hundred. It was he who was troubled about the breaking of a water main or the sudden illness of a child. It seemed that everyone came to him with their problems, no matter how small or big.

His training as a teacher came in handy for he was now dealing with great men of genius who came to him with their problems, personal and scientific, and he was both tactful and firm—never severely critical.

More and more glittering names poured in to work on one or another of the phases of trying to crack uranium. Those who had not met Oppy previously knew of his reputation, but all were amazed at his incredible instinct and vast knowledge.

When they had it all on paper and the machines were fulfilling the promises of the equations, this is what Fermi had to say about Oppenheimer: "The work certainly would have been completed without Oppenheimer, but it wouldn't have been done so soon. He was very close to being indispensable. You think someone else might have come along—but you never know."

Another scientist said this: "The main decisions were all made by Oppenheimer, and all proved to be correct. . . ."

One faulty decision would have thrown the work back perhaps months and months. To the difficulties of the project, situated as it was in New Mexico for the sake of security, there was the added handicap of getting vast tonnages of material to the isolated place on time, as needed.

Mrs. Oppenheimer says that during the final phases of the project, when it was unknown whether they were nearing success or would pull off a gigantic fiasco, Oppenheimer never slept more than four hours a night. He would be on the phone constantly, checking with branches of the project at the University of Chicago or trying to clear up a security snag with some oblivious deskman in Washington who didn't know what the project was all about.

Brother Frank, who was a research associate at the Radiation Laboratories of the University of California, was now contributing his special knowledge to the formidable team of experts. A full-fledged and respected physicist, he had done a great deal of work in cosmic rays at high altitudes and in electromagnetic isotopes. Later on he was attached to the Office of Naval Research of the Atomic Energy Commission. Now and then the brothers would phone or see each other, talk feverishly and part, patting one another on the shoulder or just grinning at each other. Frank was to go on to become a professor at the University of Minnesota from which he resigned in 1947 to devote his time to cosmic ray research.

Einstein kept in close touch with the developments and now and then President Roosevelt would be given a report.

Once Roosevelt is reported to have said wryly: "That's a lot of money—two billion dollars' worth—to entrust to a man who wears a pork-pie hat."

Incidentally, the pork pie was supposed to have become his permanent trade-mark when Oppy first arrived at Los Alamos. A security officer, the story goes, pointed to Oppy's ten-gallon hat which he enjoyed wearing and barked: "Get him something less conspicuous." Dottie, it is said, led him to a shop where he stood sadly looking at the usual hats. He picked out the most inconspicuous one he could find which turned out to be the conspicuous trade-mark.

Another story, among hundreds which have grown up about the fabulous project, is how General Groves selected Oppenheimer. It's apocryphal—though some of Oppy's best friends say with affection that it's true.

It seems that a Hollywood studio dreamed up the idea of a film at the outset of the war in which the United States manufactures an atomic bomb and wins hands down. The studio, as required by war regulations, queried the War Department on the theme. Washington gave a firm "no," and the picture of the star who was slated to be the scientific genius fell into the hands of General Groves. The star was Hume Cronyn and it is said that Groves thereafter went about looking for a scientist who would resemble the picture!

Today, both Kitty and Oppy look back on those sad, mad, desperate days at Los Alamos with something resembling nostalgia. The whole community seemed touched with a dedicated magic. It seemed as though everyone—from simple laboratory technician to top man—drove himself without letup, and with a selflessness that is rare. Some of the men broke down under the strain of day-and-night work. No one bothered about beauty parlors or haircuts or any of the refinements of daily living. Food was more a matter of hasty gulps or big bites into sandwiches, usually delivered from town.

At one point the breakdowns became so numerous that Oppy had a number of psychiatrists flown in to try and ease the tensions.

There were good reasons for the tensions and the breakdowns.

At first there were difficulties in obtaining ample supplies of uranium. The government, however, arranged a pact with Belgian whereby steady shipments soon began to arrive. Then a uranium strike was made in Canada—and while the source was not as rich as that in the Congo, still the ore was sent along in ample quantities.

The big thing confronting the scientists was the separation of U-238 from U-235. There were four ways of doing this, it was thought: by gaseous diffusion, thermal diffusion, electromagnetic separation and the use of the centrifuge. Each was amazingly expensive and no one cared much about that. But the big snag was that each suggested method would take a very long time to work out. Then again, no one was sure any of the methods would work. It is much too complex to explain just what these four methods consisted of and actually it would take a textbook to make a full explanation.

There were heartbreak, defeat, despair and failure after failure. Finally it was found that the gaseous diffusion process worked. It is not very difficult to explain how this works. Imagine a garden hose in the center of which is a strainer with very tiny holes. On one side of the strainer the uranium in gas form is pumped in. The U-235 molecules, because they are slightly lighter, move much faster and get through the holes more easily. Of course, many of the U-238's will slip through as well. Then the thing is strained over and over again, thousands of times, until a pure U-235 is obtained.

Once this headache was over, a new one presented itself. It was found that uranium in gas form was terribly toxic. Thus, leakproof pipes and noncorrosive pipes had to be designed.

It is worth mentioning that the "strainer" or porous plug through which the uranium in gas form flowed is one of the so-called "secrets" of the making of the atomic bomb.

The vast process for adapting the gaseous diffusion process was not done, of course, at the Los Alamos Laboratory but at a huge site at Oak Ridge, Tennessee, where more than seventy-five thousand persons worked at the separation plants. Many of the workers were completely unaware of what they were working at.

At Oak Ridge, as well, there was established a factory for the making of plutonium.

We will recall that U-238 does not fission under bombardment by neutrons. What U-238 does is to absorb the neutron, get a kind of indigestion and resolve itself into a new isotope known as U-239.

This newly made U-239 becomes very unhappy and every twenty-three minutes about half of it develops into an isotope of element No. 93. No. 93 is called neptunium and it is known familiarly—and for short—as NP. Well, NP-239 is unhappy, too, and every fifty-six hours half of it turns into an isotope of still another new element called plutonium. It appeared that both U-235 and Pu-239, as plutonium is called, were both pretty good as basics of the atomic bomb.

Plutonium won out by more than a neck simply because it was easier to make than to turn out U-235 in pure form through the tedious separation process of gaseous diffusion. Too, with plutonium, the physicists found a way to set up a controlled chain reaction rather than one which would go headlong.

In order to deceive the curious, atomic research at the University of Chicago was carried on under the name of the Metallurgical Laboratory. There, distinguished scientists continued research, which had begun at Columbia University, in developing a chain reaction.

The project consisted of trying to formulate a design

of graphite carbon blocks with pieces of uranium, which earlier experiments had shown to be promising. The staff soon became so huge that the project took over a brewery and began to spill over into what was the Midway of the Chicago World's Fair. They even took over the squash courts at the University of Chicago Stadium.

Then on the evening of December 2, 1942, an important and dramatic episode took place. Some fifteen distinguished scientists, among them Fermi and Dr. Alfred H. Compton, winner of the Nobel prize for physics, gathered to watch a little experiment on the squash court.

There, on the court, were blocks of graphite interspersed with uranium. Through the center of this were strips of cadmium, a tin-white metallic element.

Slowly, the strips of cadmium were pulled out and the men kept their eyes glued on the neutron counter. At first the reaction was slight, then the machine went crazy clicking up neutrons. The machine then became frenetic and began toting neutrons like mad. The first chain reaction in history had been achieved as the machine recorded the amazing number of neutrons which were picked out.

The dignified scientists also went crazy and hooted like small boys. Someone brought out a bottle of wine and a celebration was held right then and there. Today there is a metal marker on the squash court to mark the spot.

Following the making of the first pile, it was decided to build a huge factory where ample amounts of plutonium could be developed. This was constructed at Hanford, in the state of Washington, and soon some seventy-five thousand people were at work there.

Naturally, there were questions which even the greatest scientists couldn't answer. How could they be sure that the design for the plutonium factory would be the right one? They couldn't know until it was built, of course.

Another question was: How could they know what would happen to the graphite in the plutonium pile after it had been subjected to bombardment for some time? They could not answer. Yes, the explosion might be something terrific. But they couldn't know until it was built and running a while. If it did explode, well that would be unfortunate.

While all this was going on, Oppy and his crew were furiously working on the design for the bomb itself. On blueprint it looked simple, but there was just no way of knowing how much plutonium or U-235 would be needed to set it off.

Whenever scientists finished their work on other phases at Hanford or Oak Ridge, they would be assigned to help out at Los Alamos. Soon, Oppy had under him a veritable galaxy of world-famous names.

By 1944, when Oppy knew that he would soon have enough fissionable material from the Oak Ridge and Hanford plants, he began to whip himself into a frenzy of work. He knew that he would have what he needed of Pu-239 or U-235 by at least the spring of 1945.

The most formidable problem, of course, was to find out

ust how to bring the masses of fissionable material together quickly, in a one millionth of a second, so that there would be enough to make the the whole thing worth while.

Oppy's job, in effect, was to put together the weapon and to "trigger" it.

All of the material pertaining to the actual atomic bomb weapon itself is, of course, classified material and not re-easable by the Atomic Energy Commission.

But what is known is that there were two ways to set off the explosion. One way is very similar to a rifle, except that this rifle has no open end. U-235 is placed at both ends of the rifle. Nothing happens until one piece of U-235 is iterally fired, like a bullet, at the other piece. The firing s presumably done by an explosive force. When the U-235 "bullet" smashes into the U-235 target, a chain reaction takes place and there is an atomic explosion.

The second method is called implosion. This was re-ealed at a spy trial in 1951. What implosion consists of, s far as can be determined, is the placing of three dozen curved high explosives about the plutonium or U-235. When the curved explosives are set off, they also spark a chain reaction of the fissionable material.

Oppenheimer and his men finished the design and built he "gun" before they were in receipt of enough fission-ble material from Oak Ridge and Hanford.

The fissionable material arrived, the weapon was "loaded" and Oppenheimer was ready to set off the first atomic explosion in history.

8

"And Out Fell the Atom Bomb"

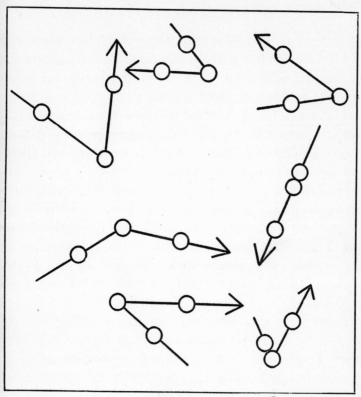

Brownian Motion

I*t was Monday, July 16, 1945. The sky was still some-*
what dark but in the east there were slender rays
beginning to poke ever-longer fingers over the desert
egion north of Alamogordo.

The day before, the greatest assemblage of distinguished

people had wound their way across the desert roads in a steady caravan. For perhaps five hundred miles about, the air and the land were being watched intently for interlopers. The war with Japan was still on.

The site had been selected by Oppy because the northwestern section of the two-thousand-square-mile Alamogordo Air Base was remote, away from towns and therefore best for security purposes.

For days the great had been assembling. Every plane that landed contained a notable. Some wore uniforms; some did not. All told, there were almost one thousand spectators. There were three hundred scientists, chemists, physicists, radiologists, meteorologists, mathematicians, explosive and ballistic experts—many of them Nobel prize winners.

There were also about two hundred and fifty military personnel who were distributed about for security purposes. There were about two hundred high officials from Washington and about two hundred high officers from the Pentagon, from the War Office in London, from Canada, Australia, China, the Philippines, Argentina, Mexico—who were the military observers for their governments and invited as a courtesy.

The roster of distinguished persons who bedded down for that Sunday night on the desert included Major General Leslie R. Groves, commander in chief of the Atomic Bomb Project; President James Bryant Conant of Harvard University and today high commissioner of Germany;

"AND OUT FELL THE ATOM BOMB"

Dr. Vannevar Bush, director of the Office of Scientific Research and Development; Dean Richard Tolman of the California Institute of Technology. Then there were Fermi, Bohr and scores of others who had for years plunged their energies into making the atomic project come true.

As the caravans rolled up and dignitary after dignitary alighted, or as planes came into the Alamogordo strip, each was led to a tent on a hill named Compania. This was set some twenty miles to the northwest of another hill which had been labeled Zero by Oppy.

It was on Zero that the first atomic blast in history was to go off.

Oppenheimer went about trying to make his guests comfortable. An old outdoor man himself, he showed how a sleeping bag could be made the most comfortable of enclosures. He strolled about to make sure that his "guests," as he called them, had had enough dinner from the rolling kitchens which had been supplied by the Army. He also saw to it that those who had been badly burnt by the desert sun were supplied with lotion.

The entire setting was an eerie sight. Searchlights were licking the sky and hunting out a gaunt tower on which the atomic bomb had been placed. Here and there, army men equipped with searchlights went about with printed instructions to be sure the observers took all necessary precautions.

There was some banter; there was much laughter; but

beneath it all, there was an uneasiness, a kind of anxiety, for each of these men knew, if even so slightly, what a successful explosion would mean in the dawn. Each was aware that he was a witness in the making of history.

Oppenheimer was very tired. Scientifically, he had lost interest in the project except insofar as improvements could be made. He had no doubts at all about the end result itself. What had showed itself to be true on paper and in the laboratory would be equally true in the field.

Bases, several miles from each other, had been erected. Oppenheimer, as scientific commander in chief, was at Base S–10, the control center.

The bomb itself was set on a structural steel tower one hundred feet high and about nine miles away from S–10.

Twice, once before bedtime which was signaled by a long blast, and again long before dawn, monitors went about in jeeps blasting instructions through loud-speakers and urging everyone to obey the rules. For example, at a long signal of the siren at minus two minutes before zero all personnel, whose duties did not specifically require them to be otherwise engaged, were to be prone on the ground immediately, the face and eyes directed toward the ground and the head away from Zero.

It is amazing how little difference there is between the first instructions to prevent radiation burns and hazards delivered before the first atomic blast, and those which the American public and its school children have been taught during the subsequent years. It is still another tribute to the

cientific precision and the methodical planning of Oppenheimer and his staff. They knew what they had and what it
ould do and how it would behave.

Youthful Dr. Joseph L. McKibben of the University of
California had the honor of setting off the first atomic
blast. He pressed no buttons as one might imagine. But
at just forty-five seconds to zero, which was set for 5:30
A.M., he set into motion a wired robot which in turn set
other robots into motion. More than five hundred miles
of wiring went into this elaborate but necessary operation.

Electronic impulses were set into motion and relayed
their messages. Then electrons, properly spaced, moved
into position at the split second.

The observers had colored film over their eyes and their
heads averted.

Overhead, two B-29 Superfortresses hovered, but so
intense was the concentration of the humans lying huddled
in their shelters, their bodies pressed in involuntary fear
against the earth, that they did not hear the drones of the
motors. The planes had been especially equipped with various recording instruments to test the reaction in the upper
atmosphere.

The operator in the radio control tower continued to
chant:

"Zero minus twenty-five seconds!"
Zero minus fifteen seconds!
Zero minus ten seconds!"

A warning flare of a deep, vivid green trailed its melancholy way across the lightening sky to warn those who might have forgotten or who might have been too fascinated. It trailed and left a pale chartreuse spume behind it

Then the giant voice from the loud-speaker on the radio blared: "Zero minus three seconds!"

And it seemed that just when the sunrise leveled itself across the roundness of the earth and came speeding westerly, there arose still another great blinding flash of light from the very innards of the earth itself—a hellish ugly, livid light that soared and swept its way and kep growing lights upon its very own lights. Then it turned green and there was a muttering and a grumbling and fantastic roaring as the neutrons assailed the nuclei and went into chain reaction without end—almost.

Up, up, up, high above the desert, higher and higher rising in a fraction of a second to eight thousand feet illuminating the sky and the earth, went the light.

The sky was aflame with light of an orange hue, changing to deep purple and then changing back again to lavender and orange as the sun came into play to create havoc with the color scheme.

The sound and the color, the depth and the dimension were like nothing seen in this world—not in earthquake or in volcanic upheavals, not in typhoons or in fierce and unrelenting storms on the seas.

The green changed rapidly to livid hues. Strange shape made up of smoke and clouds turned the sky into a si ouette out of a chamber of horrors. One man claimed he could see the outline of the Statue of Liberty. Another said he could see the Colossus of Rhodes. Still another said that he saw nothing but the form of a huge, angry fist, shaking away.

But all were in agreement that the first shape was that of a Brobdingnagian mushroom.

The mushrooming cloud went higher and higher until it reached the amazing level of forty-one thousand feet, some twelve thousand feet higher than the highest mountain on earth.

There was a hush, then a kind of vacuum of silence—and then came the roar and uproar and repeated roar of light transforming itself into sound and crashing and cascading against the distant mountains and sending back peals only to bounce back again and send back still other peals which met themselves coming and going.

There was a sudden hot blast of wind, a wind with a thick, deep smell of heat to it. It was unlike the hot desert wind which is a commonplace, but more like a wave of heat emanating from something in the stove scorched beyond recognition.

Then, as though it had been staged by an unseen hand, there came a tremendous blast of sound that rocketed, bounced and finally crumpled.

The most succinct remark of any of the observers of the new force in the life of man was made by Dr. George B. Kistiakowsky of Harvard University: "I am sure," he said,

"that at the end of the world—in the last millisecond o
the earth's existence—the last man will see what we saw.'

Someone else said facetiously but with a kind of under
standing horror: "The sun can't hold a candle to it."

But while all this drama in sound, sight, sensation and
terror was taking place, Oppenheimer and his staff had
placed strategic cameras in various spots to measure the
amounts of energy which had been released, the intensity
of the blast, the explosions which came after the blast
radiation effects in the air and on the ground, and even at
attempt to take photos of what happened inside the bomb
itself. Such is science. It always tries. However, at fiv
thousand degrees Fahrenheit, the cameras failed. It wa
not their fault.

Like some fabled, dedicated suicides in a science-fiction
story, several of Oppy's scientists at the time of the blast
were crawling toward Zero in Sherman tanks especially
lined with lead to prevent radiation hazards.

When all the noise and terrible sky lights were over
the scientists, by means of special scoops, took earth test
to see the effects of radiation on the surface of the earth
These scoops were especially manipulated from the inside
of the tanks—still another chore Oppy's fantastic projec
had thought of long before the possibility of splitting the
atom efficiently had come to pass.

But while the test itself was a shattering experience in
the hearts and the minds of those who had come to experi

nce a success, the amazing, detailed arrangements long
before the test took place would in themselves make wonderful stories in heroics. The interesting aspect of these
side stories is that scientists are not supposed to be as brave
as football players or to have their verve and aplomb. Yet
those who engaged in several of the preliminary and necessary experiments were the greatest heroes of any time. No
one but Oppy, whom they worshiped, could have gotten
them to do it. They knew he would join them gladly if the
United States government would have allowed him to
do so.

For example, there was a moment on July 3, 1945—
a story that has not been told—when a group of young
physicists "worked" up an atomic fission to a point where
it might have killed them and many others for miles about
them. However, it did not, simply because Oppy had confidence in his equations.

These young scientists—and it is perhaps one of the most
dramatic stories ever to be told—set a neutron going. If it
could not have been stopped in time, this would never have
been written. But it was stopped. The active material was
brought to a halt just before the exploding stage.

Too, another adventure in the new saga of atomic energy
involves the transportation of the atomic bomb from Los
Alamos to Zero Hill, a matter of two hundred miles.

There were two questions involved in this moving
problem. One was security, the other safety. Both were

in the hands of Captain Thomas O. Jones, in charge of Military Intelligence at Los Alamos and a former lawyer from Chicago.

When the results of the test were in, it was found that all life within a radius of one mile had been killed, including hard-to-kill rattlesnakes which hugged the ground. The steel rigging tower, weighing thirty-two tons, had been twisted into a child's toy, much of it vaporized, and the sand, within a radius of four hundred yards had become a glasslike substance, the color of pale jade.

In Amarillo, Texas, about four hundred and fifty miles east of Zero Hill, the residents phoned the police that they had seen and heard some kind of bomb go off.

Lastly, a herd of antelope, which was known to frequent the area, was never seen again.

9

Why Oak Ridge Didn't Die

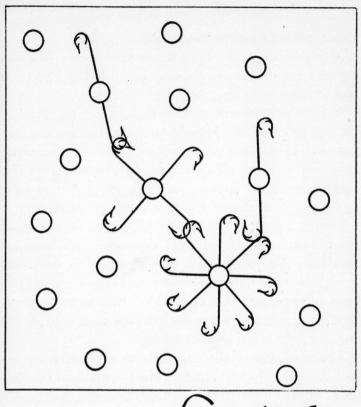

Lucretius

Chances are, you've never heard of health physics. Chances are, too, you've never stopped to think about the radiation hazards that meant either immediate death or slow, agonizing growth of cancerous tissue to the thousands of workers at Oak Ridge where the uranium piles were built for the Big Bomb.

Without health physics, a brand-new science which developed as atomic research developed, the Big Firecracker would never have been realized.

You've never heard of Fish Pole, X-22, the Paintpail Chang, Eng and the Hoople Counter, but these curious instruments, shielded behind the anonymity of their aliases, kept the workers and scientists in radiation areas from bombardment by alpha, beta and gamma rays—which might mean sure death or, at best, horrible burns.

During the eight most hazardous years of the atomic energy enterprise—from 1943 through 1950—hazardous because so little was known, only two persons were killed by radiation in laboratory accidents. In one of the accidents eight other persons were exposed to radiation, but all recovered. In two later mishaps five persons were injured, four burning their hands and one his leg.

The two accidents that caused death occurred when men in a laboratory were experimenting with large amounts of the kind of material that explodes in atomic bombs. The amounts of material being worked with were harmless if kept separate, but if brought close together, and kept together, they would throw off a great deal of harmful radiation.

Both accidents occurred in the same way—two masses of material, harmless separately, were jammed close together. In one case, one man was killed by heavy nuclear radiation; in the other, one man was killed while eight others were exposed but recovered.

The case in which four persons suffered radiation burns occurred after a weapons test when they handled radioactive material without using the protective devices available to them. In the fifth case, a worker spilled some radioactive liquid on his leg—and despite instructions, failed to remove the wet clothing promptly.

Several physicists within the past several years have developed cataracts of the eye as a result of exposure to radiation while working with cyclotrons. Since cataracts, which are a clouding of the eye lenses, do not develop until three or four years after exposure, it was difficult for the health-physics experts to determine under what conditions the damage occurred.

Before going on to discuss various aspects of radiation, it may be wise to explain just what radiation is. Radio waves are radiation. So is light. But the word radiation, as used in atomic energy programs, applies to one particular kind of radiation: nuclear radiation.

Radiation constantly strikes the earth from outer space in the form of cosmic rays. Frequently, stones in buildings contain radiation but these are not dangerously radioactive.

One of the radiations thrown off by atoms in atomic fission is the same kind that causes them to fission in the first place—the neutron, about which we have already heard a great deal.

But like uncontrolled fire or electricity that is used carelessly, nuclear radiation can be a very dangerous thing. The explosion of the atomic bomb, which releases tremendous amounts of radiation, can kill and injure thousands of persons.

Exposure to excess radiation can cause cancer. Some kinds of radiation can penetrate inside the body and overexposure to these can damage the vital organs and not only make a person ill—as thousands became ill in Hiroshima and Nagasaki—but also cause death. If a person gets too much radioactive material inside his body through the nose, mouth or a break in the skin, severe illness or death could result.

How does excessive nuclear radiation injure? The tiny living cells in our bodies are damaged by the bombardment. The atoms of elements such as hydrogen, oxygen, carbon and phosphorus inside the cells are bound together electrically in groups called molecules. When the particles or rays of nuclear radiation strike a cell, they disturb the electrical balance of the molecules and break them up. Overexposure to radiation may have other effects on the molecules within the cell. The result of overexposure is to damage cells so that they cannot do their normal work in the body—or to kill the cell. The amount of overexposure determines the amount of damage caused.

Cells are always dying in the body and being replaced as part of the natural process of life. We become ill from overexposure to radiation only if too many cells are damaged or destroyed at one time, or are destroyed continuously in sensitive spots over a long period of time.

In a way, exposure to radiation is like exposure to heat. People live safely with heat—and with nuclear radiation—by keeping the rate of exposure low enough to be harmless.

Only when exposure is very heavy is recovery in doubt. For example, excellent recovery was made by hundreds of persons in Japan even in cases where overexposure was severe. When radioactive materials are taken into the body by any means and become lodged there, the extent of the injury and the chances of recovery depend largely on the amount and the kind of material involved. Radium poisoning among watch dial painters some thirty years ago caused protracted illnesses and about twenty deaths. The watch dial workers moistened with their lips the tips of brushes that had been dipped into a phosphorescent mixture containing radium. The radium concentrated in their bones, caused bone cancer, terrible pain and, in many instances, death. Medical science could no longer help them.

While there are seven different kinds of nuclear radiation identified to date, in atomic energy programs it is customary to deal only with four: alpha particles, beta particles, gamma rays and neutrons.

Alpha particles are thrown off by radioactive elements such as radium and plutonium. They cannot damage the skin since they have very little power of penetration. Even a sheet of paper or a few inches of air can stop their progress. But they can cause intensive damage if too much of a substance that emits them gets lodged inside the body

Beta particles are thrown off by many radioactive materials—radioactive carbon and phosphorus, for example They are much smaller than alpha particles and they carry an electrical charge. They are much more penetrating than alphas and can travel several yards through the air and penetrate up to a third of an inch of tissue. Overexposure can cause very severe burns and materials that cause betas can cause great damage if they get inside the body.

Gamma rays and X rays are not particles like alphas or betas but are waves of energy such as light and radio waves. Gamma rays can travel hundreds of feet through air and penetrate for many inches through anything solid except thick lead, which acts as an effective barrier. Gamma rays are thrown off by many radioactive substances and are generated on a large scale both in atomic explosions and nuclear reactors. Oppy's brother Frank has done considerable work in the development of what we know today about rays.

Neutrons are nuclear particles with no electrical charge at all. Their mass is about one-fourth that of the alpha particle, but because they have no electrical charge they can travel many feet through solids and hundreds of feet through the air and can deeply penetrate a person's body and cause considerable havoc.

Overexposure is dependent upon how much and how

often a person is exposed to rays. For example, in using X rays on a patient a physician is careful to spread the treatment over widely separated intervals rather than using it every day. In treating cancer, overexposure is deliberate and a patient may become ill, but this cannot be helped in the fight on cancerous tissue.

Except for the few instances cited, no worker among the hundreds of thousands has been injured due to overexposure. In fact, workers at the Hanford plant averaged less exposure in a year than they would have received from a single X ray of the chest.

The rate of radiation absorption is measured in units called roentgens, named after Roentgen, the German who discovered X rays. If one hundred persons were exposed to four hundred roentgens of penetrating radiation about fifty would die of the overexposure. An X ray of a person's chest subjects him to about one-half to five roentgens. At the atomic energy plants workers are carefully checked to see that they don't average more than three tenths of one roentgen in a week. The roentgen actually applies only to the radiation of gamma rays or X rays. When a worker may be exposed to other types of radiation, the power of the other type of radiation to cause damage is interpreted in terms of the gamma power and the worker's record (a card is kept for each) is adjusted accordingly.

Each worker at Oak Ridge carried two metal cylindrical objects, like fountain pens, in his pocket. As the deathly rays bombarded, fast as thought, in billions of particles, the objects would discharge the rays just as does a lightning conductor attached to the house. The fierce tiny stings would be simply discharged.

Those who were assigned to measure fast neutron exposures in the uranium pile buildings wore films in their gloves, strapped to the wrists, to the thighs and the brow. No matter where the rays deflected, the film told the story. Periodical checks with the film took the count, and if the saturation point had been reached, the worker was assigned to another section of the vast atomic bomb plant where rays were inactive.

At the very outset of the Big Bomb project, Dr. Alfred H. Compton, director of the Metallurgical Project, the arm that was to operate the atomic bomb assembly line in the factories, became concerned with the radiation hazards to which inexperienced workers, nonscientists mainly, would be subject. Would it be fair, Dr. Compton wondered, for men and women to be put into mortal danger from causes which they did not understand?

At several points operations were postponed so that scientists could work out methods of safety against radiation hazards. And so health-physics was born.

Departments were set up that would work singly and in unison. These were called Special Clinical, Biological, Medical and Health Physics. What was known about radiation hazards by the various sections was integrated into health physics, which was at first headed up by Dr. H. M. Parker at Oak Ridge. Later, Dr. Parker transferred to Hanford and was replaced at Oak Ridge by Dr. Karl Z. Morgan of the Monsanto Chemical Company.

Health physics got to work. The new plants were inspected as to thicknesses of shields; ventilating systems were whipped up to decontaminate the air from radioactivity. A personnel monitoring system was set up to supervise each worker, to check him in and out, to watch his health and the safety equipment provided for him.

A unique laundry, the like of which the world has never seen, was established within the plants. Each article of clothing, from brassieres to shoelaces to shorts to panties, were washed in special ray-decontaminating chemicals, then each was passed through a gantlet of fantastic counters that recorded with flickering needles whether the articles were ray free.

The health physics service snooped into every corner with counting devices, locating the danger spots, setting up warning signs.

Special masks were worn. Automatic sirens geared to ray beams on a rampage would scream warnings. The masks were donned by workers and danger areas evacuated while emergency ray-decontamination squads went to work. An average working hour was a scene out of a Buck Rogers strip.

Sometimes a man might get his full potential of danger

ray in a fraction of a minute, and workers soon formed the habit of learning to check their own films and discharge condensers.

Each day the personnel monitoring section would examine the pocket discharge meters, develop the films and cast up their charts. The workers, it was found, were more easily persuaded to watch their films if they were taped to the hands and feet, a kind of inner psychological reminder.

The health physics section included about two hundred and fifty chemists, engineers and physicists. Trained men were hard to find who could be entrusted with the health supervision of the bomb workers and the operation of more than twenty main secret defensive instruments. The War Department has not yet given permission to release to the scientific journals the plans for the electrical counters, and reports from Germany indicate that, among other things, the development of the Nazi fission process was halted because of radiation hazards to the machine operators.

Dr. Morgan declares that health physics is here to stay if only because the nuclear research is continuing.

"When nuclear energy is used in the university laboratories for research, in hospitals for cancer and therapy treatment, in industry for power production and in various phases of operations of the chemical, petroleum and steel industries all over the world, there will be an even greater need for constant vigilance and extreme caution.

"When we realize that we are working with radiation

evels that could give a man a fatal radiation dose in a few
econds and with radioactive poison elements that are
atal when one millionth of a gram is fixed in the human
ody, we are led to understand the importance of health
hysics. One serious mistake could lead to an explosion or
o the contamination of a large area about the plant."

On May 21, 1946, Dr. Louis Slotin, thirty-five-year-old
uclear energy genius, and seven other physicists and scien-
ists of the Los Alamos Atomic Bomb Laboratory were
njured while working with fissionable material when
hey were exposed to radiation. It happened in a flash. On
May 30th Dr. Slotin was dead after nine days of constant
orture. The others lived—but only because Dr. Slotin
dispersed the material at the time of the accident and thus
revented greater injury to fellow scientists," in the words
f Dr. N. E. Bradbury, director of the Los Alamos project.
To quote Dr. Morgan:

"We believe that money and time spent in health physics
o prevent the contamination of our cities and to minimize
uffering and death of persons in this nuclear energy field
s a worth while investment.

"We admonish persons who plan to work with radio-
ctivity to develop the proper respect for this penetrating
adiation and we would like to invite young men and
vomen to consider entering this field of health physics
s a profession."

Scientists are notoriously close mouthed and discreet. There is a hint of how we may yet defend ourselves against enemy atomic explosions in what Dr. Morgan says about "contamination of our cities . . ." and without question health physics will be the science that will do it, if it can be done.

10

Prometheus Unbound

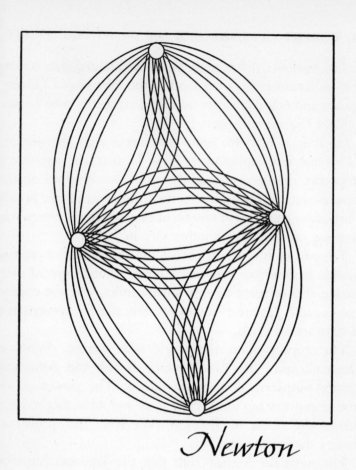

Newton

ꓳ*nce a man called Prometheus stole fire from the heav-*
ens in order that man might have light and comfort.
He was forever thereafter punished by the gods for
is impertinence. They chained him to a rock where daily
is liver was pecked at by cruel birds.

141

The dilemma of Prometheus, an earthbound man feeling only devotion to his own kind, is the dilemma of Oppenheimer and other sensitive and kindred spirits who helped to make the atomic bomb.

On August 6, 1945, just a few weeks after the successful atomic test explosion in New Mexico, the equivalent of twenty thousand tons of dynamite was dropped on the Japanese city of Hiroshima in the form of an atomic bomb. Three days later another bomb of even greater potency was dropped on Nagasaki, another city in Japan.

The loss of life was frightful and the injuries were too terrible to describe. Property damage, though spread over a wide area of some twenty square miles, was not expensive because Japanese homes are not usually constructed of stalwart materials.

The impact upon the world was terrific. Winston Churchill said: "By God's mercy British and American science outpaced all German efforts. The possession of atomic powers by the Germans at any time might have altered the result of the war. We have had profound anxiety during the race."

The news on August 10th that the Japanese Imperial Government was suing for peace did not seem as important, newsworthily, as the fact that the atom had been cracked, that atom bombs had been dropped and that the atomic age had come upon man.

The surrender of Japan was anticlimactic. What was important—and the newspapers and magazines and the peo le of the world realized it—was the fact that atomic energy, a new and mysterious force, had made its appearance.

It was much later on that the experiment in the New Mexico desert became a releasable story. And much later than that, the fragmentations of the Los Alamos project and the part played by Oppenheimer began to sift into the public prints.

But when Oppenheimer saw his first bomb cascade up from the earth and into the heavens, he felt, as he recounted later, as "if the radiance of a thousand suns were to burst at once into the sky, that would be like the splendor of the Mighty One . . . I am become death, the shatterer of worlds."

This quotation from a Hindu philosopher came to him as he watched with red-rimmed eyes, his body and his spirit drooping, the soaring, terrible majesty of the first atomic holocaust.

He had a tremendous sense of guilt and he wondered if he were right, if he were wrong—or if he were just a tool in the hands of history.

It is part of the sense and sensibility of the ethic of Western Christian civilization that men can debate this way with themselves. It is only when men lose that ethic that they no longer debate. For example, had the German Nazis arrived at the engineering feat of the splitting of the atom, they would have had no qualms of conscience at all.

But for years, long before the Los Alamosists knew

whether they could achieve the hurry-up feat, there ha
been interminable arguments about the ethics of so terri
ble a weapon.

Oppenheimer put it this way at one time: "In som
crude sense which no vulgarity, no humor, no overstate
ment can quite extinguish, the physicists have known sin
and this is a knowledge they cannot lose."

This statement was made not long after the sudder
terror and death of Hiroshima and Nagasaki.

However, an old teacher of Oppy's at Harvard Uni
versity put a more empirical ground under what th
physicist does:

"Scientists aren't responsible for the facts that are i
nature. It's their job to find the facts. There's no con
nected with it—no morals. If anyone should have a sens
of sin, it's God. He put the facts there."

Thus the solid pragmatist. Other realists argued that th
atomic bomb as a war weapon was no worse, morally, tha
a stone or a sword. "Is it more of a sin to kill one man at on
fell blow than a million?" They argued about the quantita
tive merits of sin.

Oppenheimer belongs to that school of idealistic scien
tists who believe that what emanates from the laborator
and the schoolroom should be helpful to mankind. Toda
he sees no moral problem involved in the dropping of th
bomb on Japanese cities.

"Our enemies appeared formidable and the cause i

which we were engaged seemed by no means assured of victory," he says.

However, not long after the war was over, Oppenheimer resigned from the Los Alamos project. His explanation was that he was not an "armaments manufacturer."

This statement indicates that he did not like the drift the use of atomic energy was taking. He soon found himself in the position of being the troubled voice of the physicists who had made the bomb possible and who were worried lest the thing they had unleashed would become a Frankenstein monster which would devour the world.

It was simply impossible for him to slide out from under the project and the bomb. Try as he might, he found himself more and more immersed in affairs dealing with atomic energy, atomic projects, persons in the atomic energy field, international control of atomic energy, Washington officialdom and the beginnings of the so-called "cold war" with Soviet Russia.

Constantly he found himself being drafted by the government, a chore and responsibility he could not evade even if he wished.

Although he tried to bury himself in his professorships at the University of California and Cal Tech, he found that his phone was constantly ringing and it was always a call from Washington. It was apparent that he had set a force into motion which was making history and he was one of the prime movers of that epoch.

He appeared dozens of times before Congressional hearings where he had patiently to explain to congressmen, lawyers or businessmen the implications of atomic energy. He also served on advisory boards with the War and State Departments as well as special committees set up by the President to examine the implications of the new force which had been deposited upon the international scene and was daily being used as a diplomatic weapon.

For some two months he willingly worked on a report on whether atomic energy should be made internationally useful. For this, he came in for much criticism. Like Einstein, he was and is greatly opposed to secrecy in all scientific advances. To him, science is international and transcendental.

"Secrecy," he said repeatedly, "strikes at the very root of what science is and what it is for."

One of his favorite stories to illustrate this point is that not long after the dropping of the bombs on Hiroshima and Nagasaki—and when the Japanese had surrendered—he received cables of congratulations from scientists in Japan.

"See?" he says, "science knows no national barriers."

Oppy's idealism, however, has a far more practical side. For example, he says that if the elimination of atomic weapons means the business of "going back to a good clean war," he is violently opposed. He would like to think of atomic bombs as being so mutually suicidal as to keep nations from going to war against each other.

Following the end of the war, Oppy went on several

lecture tours to try and educate the people on the meaning of atomic energy and on its implications in the event of an atomic war. He did this not because he enjoyed lecture tours but because he felt it his duty to do so.

His name had become synonymous with the A-bomb, as it had then come to be called, and there was hardly anyone who had a question on the meaning of atomic energy, or on its international implications, who did not call upon him to answer.

He delivered more than two hundred lectures in the period from the dropping of the bomb on Hiroshima to November, 1947, a space of two years. A classic example is when he appeared before a fairly literate audience at Cooper Union, the excellent school of science in New York City.

Before him there was an audience of about two thousand people. There were some professors, some advanced students, but the remainder was a cross section of America—people who can read and write, who had been overwhelmed by the implications of the atomic bomb and its threats and wanted to know what it was all about.

As he stared down at the sea of faces below him, he had a sense of pity and a feeling that there was something terribly awry with a civilization where only a handful of people knew the significance of the influences which would have tremendous impact on the hundreds of millions.

At first he began slowly to try to explain. But as idea

upon idea crowded upon his consciousness, he found himself going along at a headlong pace. He talked for about an hour without waiting to hear a reaction from the audience.

When it did come, he knew he had failed. The audience was fascinated but didn't know what he was talking about. Someone rose and asked a question and Oppy, always honest, said: "I'm sorry, you don't know enough to ask a question like that." The audience cheered. After that, he tried again.

He asked for a blackboard and tried to give a simple explanation of atomic energy and what it might mean to industry, to medicine, to agriculture. There was a silence—and when he had finished there was a burst of whistling and cheering.

It was apparent that the people did not understand—even those who were interested enough to attend lectures. One man got up and asked a question and the audience cheered again when Oppenheimer said quietly: "I'm sorry, I don't know the answer to that."

Science had outstripped the common man; its products were in the hands of people who understood it and were in awe of it but wished to use it as a weapon.

Life soon became very complex for Oppenheimer. During 1947 he found that he had made fifteen transcontinental flights to Washington from California and back. He was tired, as he put it, of "living in planes."

He resigned from his professorships at the University of

California and Cal Tech and was glad to accept the direcorship of the Institute for Advanced Study at Princeton.

Quietly, Kitty and he shut up their home in California and took residence at Olden Manor.

Meantime, despite the alarms of the atomic bomb and he fears of the new force which was let loose on the world, he atomic age of Oppy was beginning to show promise n many areas of human goodness.

He had no need to worry. No man who wears a pork-pie at, smokes a pipe, speaks eight languages, has a good ppetite and has ushered in a new age could have done nuch damage to the world he lives in.

11

Frankenstein or Friend?

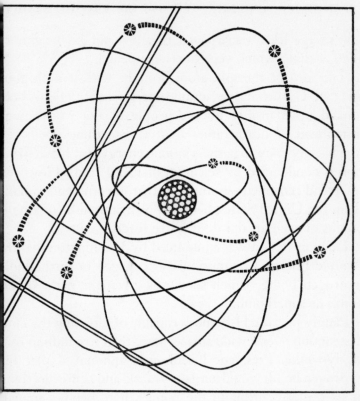

Uranium

Oppenheimer *will be the first to agree how heartbreak-*
ing it is that atomic energy came into being via a
bomb rather than through a desire to benefit all man-
ind, to lighten his work burdens and to help his illnesses.
t was as though the Stone Age had its beginnings when

one savage used a sharpened rock to split his neighbor'
skull, a thing which very likely happened.

The idea of the split atom brought with it both good
and evil. Unfortunately, atomic energy since 1945 has been
looked upon mainly by the people of the world as an
instrument of death rather than as something good.

This tendency to harness atomic energy just for destruc
tion is condemned by scientists of many lands. However
the trend remained—so much so that governments, among
them the United States, began to plan and push for atomic
bombs of even greater destructive force.

Early in 1951 it was announced by Washington that the
Atomic Energy Commission was engaged in furthering a
hydrogen bomb, which soon was given the name of H
bomb or superbomb.

Plainly put, the H-bomb is capable of effecting the same
destruction over a wide area as more than five million ton
of dynamite. President Eisenhower announced that the
hydrogen bomb would actually frazzle and sear everything
in its explosive orbit to the point where people, animal
and structures would all be vaporized. This is a horrible
picture and the stories trickling through confirmed the
bomb's terrifying power.

The first test of the H-bomb took place late in 1952 and
some of the secrecy about which it was wrapped began
to be dissipated.

The concept of the H-bomb goes back to the thirties
and its originator was Dr. Hans A. Bethe, a Cornell Uni-

versity physicist. Dr. Bethe puzzled over the sustained source of the vast amounts of energy released by the sun. He soon became very sure that the energy sent forth by the sun came from nuclear reactions. It is a known fact that the sun contains hydrogen and that its atoms constantly assail each other and set up constant chain reactions.

Dr. Bethe then struck on what is known as the Bethe Cycle. Unlike the process where a uranium atom is split in order to fashion energy, in the case of hydrogen, four hydrogen atoms get together and become one single helium atom. The business takes quite a while, Bethe estimated, merely about two hundred thousand years. That is why the label "cycle" was fastened on his theory.

But how was man to duplicate the fantastic heat of the sun in order to arrive at the same conditions? Moreover, it would take about a million years or so if the process were to be repeated on earth, while man, anxious to make wars, can't wait until four hydrogen atoms will at their own convenience bump together to form the helium atom. Splitting a helium atom does make energy, but in order to do so you would need just about the same amount of energy to set it off as you would get out of it. Anyhow, simulating the sun's temperature, which is estimated at about twenty millions degrees Centigrade, sounds like a tall order. But the concept was there and it needed only the fashioning of the atomic bomb and more knowledge and confidence for scientists to go ahead and try to rival the fury of the sun. They apparently have succeeded.

The H-bomb plant is located at Aiken, South Carolina on the shores of the Savannah River. There, in addition to turning out plutonium, as at the Hanford, Washington plant, the billion-dollar factory is also turning out tritium which is used in conjunction with hydrogen isotopes. Researchists found early that the convenient types of hydrogen made available by nature did not work at all. However they were able to isolate an isotope which, in conjunction with tritium, makes the biggest bang in the world. Tritium, by the way, is made very much the same way as plutonium, but lithium, a very light element, is used as its base rather than uranium.

It is pointless to stress just how incredibly furious would be the explosion of a hydrogen bomb over a big city such as Philadelphia or New York. The smallest of the hydrogen bombs would do damage over an area of some sixty square miles. This would include the suburbs of many big cities, of course, in addition to total destruction of downtown areas.

Suffice it to say that an entire island in the Pacific Ocean was completely wiped out by the explosion of an H-bomb having the force of five million tons of TNT. This may be compared to the atomic bomb over Nagasaki which had the force of a mere twenty thousand tons.

Following the announcement of the H-bomb experiment in the Pacific, Fermi said succinctly: "Life may become less happy from now on, but it will not be terminated." And then to set people's fears at rest, he added:

'We still don't have anything powerful enough to destroy the planet."

Oppenheimer reacted with alarm to the continued veil of secrecy put about the atom and its potentials. He called upon President Eisenhower to let the people know the facts and the implications about atomic energy as a military weapon and the plans for the use of the atomic stock piles.

"It is true that this is a dangerous world. I do not think that the dangers can be abated by keeping our people and officials in ignorance," he said. His recommendation was considered of such startling importance that the story about it ran on the front page of the newspapers of the world press. Such is his stature, however, that those who disagreed with him did not attack him as they might have another man who made the same statement.

"I have a sense of impending disaster and a sense of frustration . . . . [I doubt] that any group of people, even clever people, can find devices or tricks to cope with these problems unless they are an informed and courageous people. These are not personal problems." Then he added: 'They involve all our destiny. No one can be steward for an ignorant people. It has to do with seeing in their true somberness the dangers we have to face: war and destruction."

What Oppy wants is for the people to be let in on the intended use of the bombs and to be told what they would be in for rather than to have them rely on rumors, sensational stories and downright fabrications. By this he does not mean that the remaining secrets about the process of making the bomb should be disclosed by any means. He just wants what he calls "more candor" from the government. He thinks people are adult enough to be told the truth about the dangers they face.

But while concerned people are greatly aware of the menace of the bomb, other equally concerned people are pushing to apply atomic energy to good purposes. There are more than hopeful signs that private industry will soon be using the energy for peace. Meantime, the Navy Department got under way a program to build the first atomic-powered submarine to be named the *Nautilus*. After a "dry" run at Arco, Idaho, where the atomic engine worked smoothly and beautifully, under the direction of then Captain, now Rear Admiral H. G. Rickover, the *Nautilus* is practically ready to get wet.

It will run for years without refueling. Meantime, two more atomic-powered submarines are off the drawing boards and ready to be built. There has been some talk and rumor about an atomic-powered plane but nothing, as yet, has reached the blueprint stage.

It would be wonderful to report that atomic energy has been seized upon by many fields of endeavor and used as man's servant. But unfortunately this is not so. The greatest reason, of course, has been the secrecy about it and the monopolistic hold of the government. This is not to imply criticism; it is merely a statement of fact.

Yet already in many areas atomic energy and its by-products are being put to constructive, rather than destructive, uses. For example, a real "time detective" was erected by Dr. Willard F. Libby, a physicist of the University of Chicago. What has this "time detective" done? It determined the age of trees long ago carbonized; it placed the age of a pair of sandals found in an Oregon cave as having been made nine thousand years ago; and it said unerringly that a bison bone found in Texas belonged to an animal which was roaming the continent over nine thousand, eight hundred years ago.

How can this time machine do this? The idea for the clock goes back some time before the atom was split. Scientists, who were studying cosmic rays pouring in through the ionosphere from outer space, began to try and find out what happens upstairs. They found that cosmic rays set free neutrons which in turn changes nitrogen into radioactive carbon. Dr. Libby, armed with this, was able to work the proportion of ordinary carbon in the air to radiocarbon.

Now people, animals and plant life contain, when they are alive, the two kinds of carbon in the same proportion as they occur in the air. When a person or a plant or an animal dies, no more carbon is being absorbed and the carbon clock begins to run down.

This carbon becomes radioactive. But like all radioactive atoms, radiocarbon has a short span of life. After 5568 years only about half of the radioactive carbons are left. After another 5568 years only half of that half are left, and so on. So after about 25,000 years only about one thirtieth of radioactive carbons are still emitting rays—and this is too small for the machine to measure. This means that the machine is amazingly accurate at guessing ages if something is not more than about 25,000 years dead.

What is the value of such a clock? It is of extreme value to specialists in natural history, to archaeologists, to Egyptologists and others fascinated with the ancient past.

This gives but an infinitesimal notion of what will be achieved by the use of atomic energy and atomic developments once the atom is used for peace and not for war.

Oppy, a cultured man, would have preferred saying "We shook the tree of knowledge and out fell atomic energy for the use of mankind"—instead of "and out fell the atomic bomb."

There is the story of the man who lay dying of a brain tumor at the Massachusetts General Hospital. Into his veins were injected a phosphate solution containing radioactive atoms of phosphorus. After waiting a day, the doctors began to "prospect" for the hidden tumor with a special, needle-thin Geiger counter wired to an electronic totaling machine.

Brain tumors have a special affinity for phosphorus and collect it in greater concentration than surrounding normal tissue. If there were a growth in the man's brain, then it would show up as a signal on the atomic scoreboard. It did. It showed up in the narrow, central lobe known as the vermis. No surgical probe would have done it. The doctors exposed the brain, found the tumor just where the counter said it would be, operated and saved the man's life.

From all over the world there come cries for isotopes, those radiating piles turned out at Oak Ridge and Hanford. Mercy planes take off daily bearing this by-product on behalf of cancer-ridden people, hyperthyroids and even those ill with leukemia, a blood ailment.

Radioactivity is being used to aid in the study of anemia, for some children lack sufficient red blood corpuscles so necessary to life and vigorous living. Radioactive phosphorus is being used to study blood flow to the heart and to find out what happens when a blood clot blocks the pathway to the heart and causes coronary occlusion, that sudden killer.

As in the case of the man with the brain tumor, radio-isotopes are invaluable to researchers and doctors in probing inner recesses of a body where they could not take a look without operating. For example, injecting radioso-dium into the blood stream can reveal the degree and rapidity of blood circulation a sick person has. The process is simple. A sample of the blood is taken and then an analysis is made to see how "watered" down the radio-activity is, an extremely valuable tool in the diagnosis of poor blood circulation. There have been instances where men and women in traffic accidents have been spared the amputation of an arm or a leg when the doctors were able to determine whether the blood was still circulating through the injured limbs.

There are good hopes that the food supply of the world can be improved and the lands made to flourish better by the use of a radiotracer which can inquire into the operations of plant life and growth. Through the tracer, it can be determined how much or how little fertilizer is needed. The same techniques applied to human beings with the aid of isotopes can also be used to make healthier cattle and pigs. And this, too, will step up the food supply of a hungry world.

One fascinating experiment was made with flies, the ubiquitous pest known all over the world and which carries disease with it. Some fifteen thousand flies were denied water, and when they were good and parched they were given dosages of radioactive phosphorus solutions. They were then given their freedom and flytraps were laid in a radius of about twelve miles from the point of release. The traps, of course, were baited with decaying meat. Flies were gathered at those trap points and they were all the radioactive flies which had just been released. What did it prove? It showed how far and how fast flies can migrate to sources of filth and decay, a help in mapping out fly-riddance programs.

Radioactivity is also used to insure fresh and wholesome foods and drugs which are inclined to breed disease germs. Irradiation is used, for example, on milk and milk products and some of the newer antibiotics before they are sealed into their containers or bottles. The same idea is being applied in many instances at canning plants.

In industry, radioactivity is being used to measure the wear and tear from friction in machines without the need for dismantling them. Parts of motors which have a tendency to wear out are coming under the sharp, inquiring glance of radioactivity to see how their components can be made better.

In the oil fields, in the rubber tire factories, radioactive measuring devices are also being used to take a look into the oil and the rubber, to make for improved products.

The Atomic Energy Commission has sent shipments of isotopes to thirty-eight nations for about fifteen hundred different types of users. More than thirty-five thousand distinct shipments have been made. Meanwhile, these shipments cost the taxpayer almost nothing, for the recipients, except those engaged in research in cancer and other illnesses who are allowed a discount, must pay.

It is a sad thing to say, but the several billions of dollars expended by the Atomic Energy Commission has been geared—99.9 per cent of it—to war, to the use of atomic energy for destruction. Just a mere .1 per cent has been spent on atomic radiation or energy for health, industry and agriculture.

It would be nice to report in a few years that this statistic has been stood on its head.

Oppy is still the optimist for he has great faith in the young men of science who will come after him.

He is sure that the Los Alamos adventure, which has had such a bad effect among people of sensibility because of the monster created there, will in the long run turn out to be a great and a good thing.

He consoles himself when he is, in common with other atomic scientists, afflicted with a deep sense of guilt and perhaps a stray regret. He says: "I don't see much difference in being torn to pieces by an atom bomb or gunpowder. . . ."

This, he admits, is rationalization, for he goes on to say: "The destructive possibilities of our technology has already outrun any human control. It is a very worrisome thing. It is highly ironic that science should come up with atomic energy at a time of such deep conflict. . . ."

As he broods, so brood dozens of his eminent colleagues who are fearful about the thing they have unloosed upon the world. Perhaps the man who helped usher in the Stone Age had the same misgivings.

History will know best how to evaluate whether good or evil will derive from the harnessing of atomic energy. One thing is certain, fascism was a hideous, evil thing and any weapon to destroy it, for the sake of the world and of history, was essential. Oppy shaped that weapon and for this he is a greatly honored man. For history as we know it and democracy as we know it would have been obliterated by the smash of an atomic bomb in the hands of the Fascist.

It is to Oppenheimer's honor and integrity that he expresses his concern and that he is opposed to secrecy about the aims and intentions of those who have the power to unleash the bombs. Men of good will who know history have no fear of the end of things for mankind or of the beautiful things of life. Many similar things were said of gunpowder when it first began to be used in warfare. Yet the world has survived long enough to greet the morning of the new age. There will be other mornings and brighter ones to come when atomic energy is harnessed to the plow of civilization and does man's bidding in the multiple fields of goodness.

Glossary of Words and Terms Frequently Used in Atomic Energy

Atom. The smallest particle of an element.

Atomic Energy. Energy liberated by changes in the nucleus of an atom as by fission of a heavy nucleus or condensation of light nuclei into heavier ones, with accompanying loss of mass.

Bombard. To subject a body to the assault of rays which impinge upon it.

Chain Reaction. A nuclear reaction yielding energy which in turn causes further reaction of the same kind. More neutrons are released which in turn cause further fissions which release more neutrons, which in turn split more atoms and release further neutrons, and so on.

Cosmic Rays. A ray of extremely high penetrating power produced beyond the earth's atmosphere by transmutations of atoms continually taking place through interstellar space. These rays constantly bombard the earth.

J. ROBERT OPPENHEIMER *and the* ATOMIC STORY

Element. One of ninety-six known varieties of matter.

Fission. The splitting of an atomic nucleus by neutrons. This results in the release of enormous quantities of energy when such heavy elements as uranium and plutonium are split.

Geiger Counter. A thin-walled, cylindrical tube with a needle-like electrode projecting within, which detects the passage through its walls of every ionizing particle, such as a cosmic ray particle, by the momentary current set up on ionization of the contained gas.

Hydrogen. An element commonly isolated as a colorless, tasteless, odorless gas, inflammable and lighter than any other known substance. The hydrogen atom is the simplest of all atoms, the ordinary isotope consisting of a single proton in the nucleus and a single electron outside the nucleus. It is accompanied by a minute amount of a heavier isotope called deuterium.

Implosion. A method of exploding the atomic bomb consisting of a bursting inward.

Isotope. Any of two or more forms of the same element occupying the same position in the periodic table (that is, having the same atomic number); but distinguishable by radioactive transformations and differences in atomic weight. According to present theory the nuclei of the isotopes of an element contain the same number of protons but different numbers of neutrons.

Nucleus. The central part of an atom containing most of its mass and having a positive charge equal to the atomic number of the element. The nucleus of ordinary or light hydrogen is the proton; according to present theory, all other nuclei are combinations of protons and neutrons.

Plutonium. A radioactive element formed by the decay of neptunium.

GLOSSARY OF WORDS AND TERMS

Radioactivity. The process whereby such elements or isotopes, such as radium, uranium and thorium, spontaneously emit particles or rays or both because of the disintegration of the nuclei of their atoms. In this connection, artificial radioactivity may be induced by bombarding nuclei with particles, as from a cyclotron.

Uranium. A radioactive element of the chromium group found in combination in pitchblende and other rare minerals and reduced as a heavy, hard, nickel-white metal. Natural uranium consists of the isotope of mass No. 238. U-238 can be converted into plutonium which, as well as U-235, is used as a source of atomic energy.

Bibliography

The Effects of Atomic Weapons. Government Printing Office.
Semiannual Reports of the U.S. Atomic Energy Commission to the Congress of the United States. Government Printing Office.
A General Account of the Development of Methods Using Atomic Energy for Military Purposes. By H. D. Smyth. Government Printing Office.
Handling Radioactive Wastes in the Atomic Energy Program. Government Printing Office.
The Hydrogen Bomb and International Control: Technical and Background Information. Joint Committee on Atomic Energy. Government Printing Office.
Isotopes . . . a 3-Year Summary of United States Distribution. Government Printing Office.
Sourcebook on Atomic Energy. By Samuel Glasstone. New York (Van Nostrand).
Engineering Developments in the Gaseous Diffusion Process (McGraw-Hill).
Applied Atomic Power. By E. S. C. Smith and Others (Prentice-Hall).
The Atom at Work. By Jacob Sacks (Ronald Press).
Atom Smashers. By Raymond F. Yates (Didier).

171

J. ROBERT OPPENHEIMER *and the* ATOMIC STORY

Atomic Energy. By Karl K. Darrow (Wiley).

Atomic Energy in War and Peace. By Gessner G. Hawley and Sigmund W. Leifson (Reinhold).

Atomic Power. By R. Barnard Way (Wells Gardner, Darton & Co., England).

Atomics for the Millions. By Maxwell Leigh Eidinoff and Hyman Ruchlis (McGraw-Hill).

Dawn Over Zero. By William L. Laurence (Knopf).

Modern Ideas of the Atom. By S. Lucas (George G. Harrop & Co., Ltd., London).

Endless Horizons. By Vannevar Bush (Public Affairs Press).

The Story of the Atomic Bomb. By William L. Laurence (The New York *Times*, September and October, 1945).

Detectives of Time (*The Atlantic Monthly*, July, 1953).

David and His Atomic Slingshot (*Steelways*, September, 1949).

A Plea for Candor About the Atom (The New York *Times* Magazine, June 21, 1953).

The Scientists (*Fortune*, October, 1948).

Atomic Weapons and American Policy (*U.S. News & World Report*, July 10, 1953).

Will Our Cities Survive? (*Look*, June 30, 1953).

The Reactor Development Program (*Chemical and Engineering News*, August 29, 1949).

Behind the Scenes With a Genius (*The Reader's Digest*, February, 1949).

The Fetish of Atomic Secrecy (*Harper's*, August, 1953).

Oppenheimer (*Life*, October 10, 1949).

The Atom May Save Your Life (*The Saturday Evening Post*, July 8, 1950).

Ethical Culture—A Way of Life (New York *Herald Tribune*, January 25, 1953).

Explaining the Atom. By Selig Hecht (Viking).

BIBLIOGRAPHY

The New Force. By Ralph E. Lapp (Harper).

The Guarded Peak (*This Week Magazine*, November 2, 1952).

"The Man Who Built the A-Bomb" (The New York *Times* Magazine, April 18, 1948).

Atomic "Hired Hand" for the Farmer (*Science and Mechanics*, June, 1949).

The Man in the Pork-Pie Hat (*Science Illustrated*, September, 1948).

Counters (*Scientific American*, July, 1950).

Index

A-bomb. *See* Atomic bomb
Adler, Dr. Felix, 21-22, 23
Aiken, S. C., site of H-bomb plant, 156
Alamogordo Air Base, 116, 117
Alpha particles, 131-32
Anderson, Carl D., 61, 63
Arco, Idaho, Scene of atomic-powered submarine, 158
Aristotle, and theory of "elements," 77
Army Submarine Base," 101
Atom, Democritus' theory of, 76; Einstein's theory of, 86; helium, 155; splitting of, 44, 48, 70, 71, 93, 95, 106-09, 153, 155; theories pertaining to, 77-81, 91-92; weight of, 94-95. *See also* Atomic bomb; Atomic energy
Atomic bomb, 7, 64, 69, 111, 153; as diplomatic weapon, 146; enlightening people on, 157-58; ethics concerning, 143-46, 164; experiment at University of Chicago Stadium, 109; Oppenheimer heads project on, 72; "secrecy" of, 11, 102, 146; sponsored by U. S. government, 96; stockpiles of, 157; test blast of, 117-22, 142; work on, at Los Alamos, 102-03, 106, 109-11. *See also* Atom; Atomic energy
Atomic energy, educating the people on, 146-48, 164-65; Einstein's letter to Roosevelt on, 71; explanation of, 92-93; release of, 85-86, 92, 143, 145, 146; used for man's benefit, 86, 153-54, 158, 160, 161, 164-65. *See also* Atom; Atomic bomb
Atomic Energy Commission, 4, 10, 11, 104, 110, 154, 163
Atomic test explosion, 116-23, 142, 143; results of test, 124. *See also* Atom, Atomic bomb; Atomic energy

Bamberger, Louis, 7
Becquerel, Antoine Henri, 79-80
Belgian Congo, source of pitchblende, 86, 106
Beryllium, 87, 88
Beta particles, 131-32
Bethe Cycle, 155
Bethe, Dr. Hans A., 154-55
Blériot, Louis, 18
Bohr, Dr. Niels, 44, 93, 94, 101, 117
Born, Max, 44-46, 47
Bradbury, Dr. N. E., 137
Bridgman, Percy, 34-36, 42, 44
"Bullet" explosion, 111
Bush, Dr. Vannevar, 117

California Institute of Technology (Cal Tech), invites Oppenheimer to teach, 52; life at, 59-61, 145; resigns from, 148-49
Cambridge University, Oppenheimer at, 10, 43-45
Cavendish Laboratories, 43-44
Cellini, Benvenuto, 7
Centrifuge method, 106-07

INDEX

Graphite carbon blocks, 109; experiment with, 109, 110

Groves, Major General Leslie R., 72, 116; and Oppenheimer, 105

Hahn, O., experiments of, 89-90, 91

Hanford, Washington, atom plant at, 109-10, 133, 156, 161

Harvard University, Oppenheimer at, 33-37, 41, 43, 45, 65

Health physics, 127-38. *See also* Oak Ridge, Tenn.

Helium atom, 155

Hiroshima, bombing of, 130, 142, 144, 146, 147

Hitler, Adolf, 67, 68, 69, 70, 90

Hoover, J. Edgar, 70

Hydrogen, 64, 155-56, 168

Hydrogen atom, 155, 168

Hydrogen bomb, 64, 154-56, 157, 168

Implosion, explanation of, 111, 168

Industrial revolution (1904), 18

Institute for Advanced Study, 3-4, 7-9, 59-60, 149

Irradiation, 162-63

Isotope, explanation of, 94, 168; hydrogen, 156; medical uses of, 161, 163

Italy, 18; and fascism's effect on science, 48; joins Nazi Germany, 68

Japan, 18; attacks Pearl Harbor, 67, 69; bombing of, 142, 144, 146, 156; sues for peace, 142; threatens Australia, 70

Johns Hopkins University, Frank Oppenheimer gets degree at, 66

Jones, Captain Thomas O., 124

Kelly, Henry A., 23

Kennan, George F., 5

Kistiakowsky, Dr. George B., 121

Klock, Augustus, 29-31, 33, 42

Lawrence, E. O., 61

League of Nations, 46

Libby, Dr. Willard F., 159

Lithium, used in H-bomb, 156

Los Alamos Atomic Bomb Laboratory, erection of, 99-102; problems at, 105-06, 110; resignation from, 145; story of, 143. *See also* Santa Fe, N. M.

Massachusetts General Hospital, 160

McKibben, Dr. Joseph L., sets off first atomic blast, 119

Meitner, Lise, 90; and uranium experiment, 91, 92

Meson, theory of, 63

Metallurgical Laboratory, atom research at, 108-09

Metallurgical Project, 134

Millikan, Robert A., 61

Molecule, explanation of, 45-46; U-235, 107

Morgan, Dr. Karl Z., 135; on health physics, 136-38

Mycology, 10, 61

Nagasaki, bombing of, 130, 142, 144, 146, 156

Nature, British publication, 91

Naturwissenschaften, Die, 89

Nautilus, first atomic-powered submarine, 158

Nazism. *See* Fascism

Neptunium, 108

Netherlands, overcome by Nazi, 67

Neumann, John van, 5

Neutrons, dramatic experiment with, 109, 123; explanation of, 92; theory of, 87; type of nuclear radiation, 131, 132-33

New York Mineralogical Club, 25, 26

New York Times, 94

INDEX

North Atlantic Treaty Organization (NATO), 11
Nuclear fission, work on, 69
Nuclear radiation, explanation of, 129-33; at Hiroshima and Nagasaki, 130, 131; types of, 131
Nuclear reaction, 155
Nucleus, in physics, explanation of, 87, 168

Oak Ridge, Tenn., atom factory at, 107, 110, 127, 161; protecting workers at, 133-34. *See also* Health physics
O'Connell, Frank, 100
Olden Manor, 9, 149
Oppenheimer, Ella Freedman (mother), 17, 19, 20, 26
Oppenheimer, Frank Freedman (brother), 25, 30, 31, 65-66, 104
Oppenheimer, J. Robert, boyhood years of, 15-33; at Cambridge, 43-45; as director of Institute for Advanced Study, 3-4, 6-12, 59-60, 149; elected member of N. Y. Mineralogical Club, 25-27; and ethics concerning atom bomb, 143-46, 154, 164-65; at European universities, 43-49; and first atomic bomb test, 117-22; and friendship with Born, 44-46; genius of, 6, 7, 11-12, 15-25, 41-43, 51-60; at Harvard University, 33-37, 41-42; heads atomic bomb project, 72; as lecturer, 147-48; at Los Alamos, 99-114; marries Katherine P. Harrison, 61; school years of, 21-33; work as physicist, 9, 43, 45-46, 47, 62-64, 66; and years in California, 52, 57-58, 59, 61, 145, 148-49
Oppenheimer, Julius (father), 16, 19, 20-21, 26, 29
Oppenheimer, Katherine P. (wife), 9-10, 61, 64, 65, 102, 104

Oppenheimer, Peter (son), 9, 66, 102
Oppenheimer-Phillips Effect, research on, 63-64
Oppenheimer, Toni (daughter), 9

Parker, Dr. H. M., 135
Pearl Harbor, Japan attacks, 69
Periodic table, 27, 88, 89, 90
Perro Caliente, 50
Phillips, Melba, 64
Pitchblende, 86
Pliny the Elder, 7
Plutonium, 108, 109, 110, 156, 168
P. M. S., 44
Positron, theory pertaining to, 63
"Project Windshield Wiper," 101
Prometheus, 12, 141
"Protons," 79, 80

Quantum electrodynamics, 63
Quantum mechanics, application of, 45

Radiation. *See* Nuclear radiation
Radiation casualties, 128-29, 137
Radiation Laboratories (University of California), 104
Radioactive phosphorus, 160-61, 162
Radioactivity, 169; in agriculture 163; in industry, 163; in medicine 160-62
Radiocarbon, 159-60
Radiotracer, in plant life, 162
Radium poisoning, among dial painters, 131
Rickover, Rear Admiral H. G., 158
Roentgen, discoverer of X Rays, 133
Roentgens, 133
Roosevelt, Franklin D., discusses atom bomb with Churchill, 96; receives letters from Einstein, 70 renders aid to Allies, 67; sets up atomic energy committee, 71; in

178

INDEX

Set in Linotype Janson
Format by David Rosenberg
Manufactured by Montauk Book Mfg. Co., Inc.
Published by JULIAN MESSNER, INC., New York